Steck-Vaughn
careerready™
Business Writing

Steck-Vaughn®

HOUGHTON MIFFLIN HARCOURT

www.steckvaughn.com/adulted
800-289-4490

D1441532

Table of Contents

About ACT®'s WorkKeys® and the *Steck-Vaughn CareerReady*™ Series

ACT®'s WorkKeys® Job Skills Assessment System

Measuring the skills of every jobseeker is a vital part of the hiring process. Created by ACT®, the WorkKeys® Job Skills Assessment System allows you to demonstrate to potential employers that you have the essential writing skills to be successful in the workplace. Your business writing skills will be scored on a 5-point scale, with 5 being the highest score.

Prepare for the Future with *Steck-Vaughn CareerReady*™

Steck-Vaughn, long known as the gold standard in adult education, has created an exciting new series to help you prepare for the WorkKeys® Business Writing assessment. *Steck-Vaughn CareerReady*™ provides a comprehensive program to help you acquire the skills needed for successful business writing.

- **Focus on Student Needs**   The lesson format leads you through instruction with modeling and guided practice, ultimately preparing you for independent writing. Each unit focuses on one major trait of effective writing: Development of Ideas; Organization; Style and Tone; Sentence Structure; and Grammar, Usage, and Mechanics.

Online Pretest   The timed *Pretest* allows you to assess what you already know and what you need to learn. It mimics the WorkKeys® assessment.

Online Unit Assessments   You are encouraged to check your progress as you move through the series. Online *Unit Assessments* allow you to assess whether you are ready to move on or need review.

Online Posttest   The *Posttest* mimics the actual WorkKeys® test-taking experience. This test is timed and features a WorkKeys®-style writing prompt.

Online Teacher Support   There is one teacher plan for every student lesson. The teacher lesson plans provide guided instruction, additional support, and student activities.

→ Please visit **www.mysteckvaughn.com/CAREER** for more information about the online components.

Begin with the Pretest

You may complete the pretest online or on paper. Your pretest results are used to determine where you should begin your studies in this book.

The Writing Process

These pages take you through the steps of the writing process—prewriting, writing a draft, revising, and editing—that are key to writing effectively on the WorkKeys® assessment and on the job.

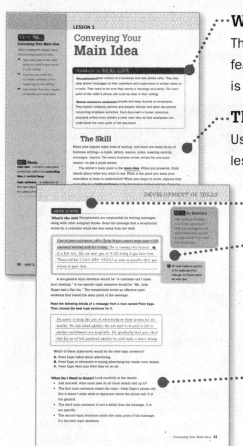

WorkKeys® in Real Life

This section provides immediate contextualization for the lesson skill by featuring two real jobs that use it. This allows you to see how each skill is applied in real life and how it could apply to your future job.

The Skill

Using clear explanations and language, the instruction portion of each lesson teaches the target concept using real-world connections.

Here's How

This page extends the instruction and is divided into two sections.

What's the Job?

This section presents a realistic job situation that requires the use of the lesson skill and an effective example of how to apply the target concept. You will be asked to answer a question related to the target concept. Sidebar features connected to this section include contextualized instruction as you work through the example.

What Do I Need to Know?

This section provides you with clues that can be used to answer the question. The answer and full explanations are immediately provided so that you may assess your understanding of the material.

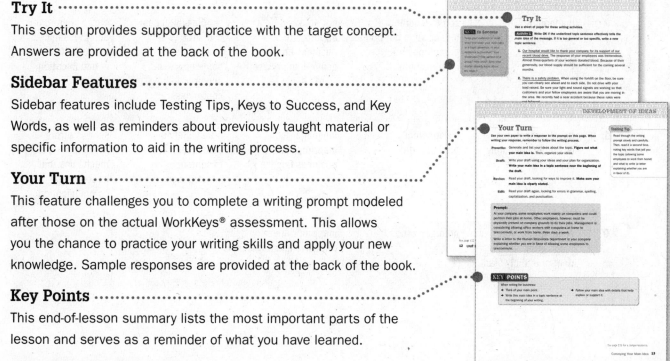

Try It

This section provides supported practice with the target concept. Answers are provided at the back of the book.

Sidebar Features

Sidebar features include Testing Tips, Keys to Success, and Key Words, as well as reminders about previously taught material or specific information to aid in the writing process.

Your Turn

This feature challenges you to complete a writing prompt modeled after those on the actual WorkKeys® assessment. This allows you the chance to practice your writing skills and apply your new knowledge. Sample responses are provided at the back of the book.

Key Points

This end-of-lesson summary lists the most important parts of the lesson and serves as a reminder of what you have learned.

Answers and Responses

You can quickly check your answers for each *Try It* practice item and review sample responses for the *Your Turn* prompts in the *Answers and Responses* section at the back of the book.

Scoring Rubric

Use the following rubric to evaluate the responses to *Your Turn* sections, the Pretest, and the Online Unit Assessments.

Score	Development of Ideas	Organization	Style and Tone	Sentence Structure	Grammar, Usage, and Mechanics
5	clear main idea; well-developed support with examples and details; keeps focus on topic; shows clear understanding of subject	organization appropriate to subject; clear paragraph structures; writing flows; skillful transitions	appropriate to audience (supervisor, coworker), business setting, and subject; varied and precise word choice	variety of sentence structures; variety of sentence lengths; effective and varied sentence beginnings	free from errors in grammar and mechanics, or with minor errors that do not affect communication
4	main idea stated and developed with supporting examples and details; keeps focus on topic	organization appropriate to subject; paragraphing; clear transitions	mostly appropriate business English; some varied word choice	generally varied sentence structures, lengths, and openings	some minor errors in grammar and mechanics that do not affect communication
3	development adequate but incomplete; general examples and limited details	organization generally clear, but some paragraphing problems; few transitions	somewhat appropriate business English but may include informal language; some imprecise word choice	limited sentence variety; some choppiness or long, rambling sentences; little variety in sentence openings	errors in grammar and mechanics that generally do not affect communication
2	inadequate development of ideas	some apparent organization but poor paragraph structure; no transitions	not always appropriate business English; general, imprecise word choice	simple sentences with little variety in length and some errors in construction; choppiness	errors in grammar and mechanics that affect communication
1	development that is simple or entirely lacking	no apparent organization	language inappropriate to business English	little variety in sentences; errors in sentence construction	serious errors in grammar and mechanics that impede clear communication
0	complete lack of focus; may be very brief or entirely blank	no organization	inappropriate or offensive language		

Pretest

Purpose

The purpose of this test is to assess your writing skills as they relate to workplace success. The writing skills assessed include development of ideas, organization, use of standard business English, sentence structure, and grammar and mechanics. You may already be proficient in some of these skills. This Pretest will assess your level of proficiency and identify which sections of the book you should study.

Test Time

You will have 30 minutes to complete the Pretest. Remember to use the writing process: generate and organize ideas, write a draft, and revise and edit the draft.

Directions

Read the writing prompt and write a response. You may use scratch paper to generate ideas and plan your paper before you begin writing.

Prompt:

Ever since a new mall was built nearby, fewer employees at your workplace are using the company cafeteria. This decreased use has created problems of waste and higher prices for those employees who eat in the cafeteria. The company is considering cutting the time allowed for lunch from 60 minutes to 30 minutes, making it difficult for employees to go to the mall for lunch.

Write a letter to the human resources department explaining why you think this policy would be fair or unfair. Give specific reasons for your point of view.

Unit Placement

Compare your Pretest response to the model response on page 112. Your instructor will use the rubric on page vi to evaluate your response. Your five scores will determine the units you need to study in this book. Begin by reviewing "Using the Writing Process" on pages 2–7. Then use the chart below to plan your course of study.

If you score 1, 2, or 3 on	Then you should study
Development of Ideas	Unit 1 (page 8)
Organization	Unit 2 (page 26)
Style and Tone	Unit 3 (page 44)
Sentence Structure	Unit 4 (page 54)
Grammar, Usage, and Mechanics	Unit 5 (page 72)

Using the Writing Process

KEYS TO...

Using the Writing Process

Keep the following points in mind:

➔ Before you begin a piece of writing, identify your topic, purpose, and audience and jot down ideas about your topic.

➔ Identify your main idea and state it in a topic sentence.

➔ Make a list, idea map, or outline of reasons, examples, or facts that support your main idea.

➔ Use your prewriting notes to write a draft.

➔ Revise and edit your draft, checking for logical organization, sentence variety, clear transitions, and correct grammar and mechanics.

KEY Words

prompt a hypothetical situation for which a writer is asked to write a response; usually used on writing tests

The Skill

When you have to write a business report; a letter or memo to your boss, coworkers, or customers; or a response to a **prompt** on the Business Writing assessment, you may feel at a loss about where to start. Using the writing process is the key to a well-written report, letter, or memo—and to a good score on the test. Following the steps of the process will help you produce a piece of writing that has the qualities of all good business writing: a clearly stated main idea, details that support the main idea, a logical organization with clear transitions between sentences and paragraphs, varied and well-structured sentences, and correct grammar and mechanics.

The writing process consists of five steps: (1) prewriting, (2) drafting, (3) revising, (4) editing, and (5) presenting the final draft. The following pages demonstrate the writing process, explaining each step by showing how a business writer might respond to the following prompt. Even though this prompt requires writing a memo supporting a position, the same writing process can be used for business reports, letters, e-mails, and other business writing. As you read, think about how you can adapt this writing process to any piece of business writing you do.

> **Prompt:**
>
> The Human Resources Department where you work has asked for your input about changing two of the current fixed paid holidays, Presidents' Day and the day after Thanksgiving, to paid floating holidays. According to the plan, offices would no longer be closed but would remain open on these holidays, and employees would be allowed to take these two paid holidays at any time throughout the year, with the permission of their supervisor.
>
> Write a memo to the director of human resources stating your opinion about changing these two holidays to floating holidays. Give reasons to support your opinion.

Prewriting

Before you begin to write, spend some time **prewriting**. Plan your writing by thinking for a moment about your topic, purpose, and audience. Then explore your ideas and identify the main point you want to make. Finally, list and organize details that support your main idea.

Identify Your Purpose and Audience First, **determine your purpose**. A prompt on the writing test will explain the purpose. It will likely be to state your opinion—in other words, to persuade. In other business writing, you must decide if your purpose is to persuade, to inform, to describe, or to explain. Your purpose affects how you state your main idea and the kind of supporting details you use.

Next, **determine your audience**. For the writing test, your audience is your scorer. In actual workplace writing, is the audience your supervisor, a client, a coworker, or a supplier? The audience affects your tone and style. You would use a more casual tone and style in a memo to coworkers about a company picnic than you would use in a proposal to your supervisor.

Explore Ideas When responding to a prompt, use a separate piece of paper to jot down as many ideas as you can think of. In other business writing, you might also explore ideas by researching business data, by interviewing, or by reading current articles related to your business.

Identify Your Main Idea Look over your prewriting notes about the topic and identify the main point you want to make. Clearly state this main idea in a complete sentence.

List and Organize Supporting Ideas Next, list the reasons, examples, or facts you will use to support your main idea. Decide on a logical organization for presenting these supporting details, such as order of importance or cause-and-effect order. The nature of your supporting details will determine the type of organization you use. In most cases, you probably will present the supporting details for your main idea in order of importance. To help organize your supporting details, you might create an outline or an idea map, like the one shown on the next page.

KEY Words

prewriting planning work done prior to beginning a piece of writing

Testing Tip

The Business Writing test may be taken online or on paper. In both situations, you are allowed to use scratch paper to plan and organize your ideas. Be sure to take advantage of this opportunity to prewrite.

The following prewriting model is based on the writing prompt on page 2.

Identify Your Purpose and Audience

- Topic: Changing two fixed holidays to floating holidays
- Purpose: To give an opinion
- Audience: Director of Human Resources

Explore Ideas

- My opinion: possibly make Presidents' Day a floating holiday but keep day after Thanksgiving fixed
- Background knowledge: What kinds of companies are closed on Presidents' Day? on day after Thanksgiving? Would my company receive many calls or requests on Presidents' Day? on day after Thanksgiving?
- Personal side: How do employees feel about having Presidents' Day off? the day after Thanksgiving off? How are they affected?

Identify Your Main Idea

- I recommend that we make Presidents' Day a floating holiday and keep the day after Thanksgiving as a fixed holiday.

List and Organize Supporting Details

Presidents' Day	day after Thanksgiving
few clients closed	many clients closed
typical number of phone calls	few phone calls
employees prefer floating holiday for family needs	employees prefer fixed holiday and would take day off anyway

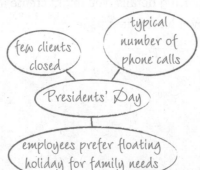

Drafting

Refer to your prewriting notes as you write a **first draft**. State your main idea in the introductory paragraph and give a brief preview of your supporting details. Begin a new paragraph for each major point and elaborate on your supporting facts, examples, or reasons. Then end your draft with a concluding paragraph that sums up your piece of writing.

Do not worry too much about making errors in spelling or grammar at this stage. You will take time to find and fix them in a later step.

KEY Words

first draft the first piece of writing based on prewriting notes

Model of First Draft

In response to your request for my input, I recomend that we make Presidents' Day a floating holiday and keep the day after Thanksgiving a fixed holiday. I base my opinion partly on the holiday policies of our client ❶ companies. I also considered how our employees feel about the issue. These policies and sentiments support treating the two holidays differently. ❷

Changing Presidents' Day to a floating holiday makes sense. Most ❸ of our client companies conduct business on this day. Because we receive a typical number of phone calls and service requests, closing our office is disruptive for our clients. Most of our employees state that their families do not have this day off. For this reason, they would prefer a floating holiday to use when they can spend time with there families. Employees could also time their floating holiday to coincide with a school holiday. So finding child care on such a day would be unnecessary. ❹

The day after Thanksgiving should remain a fixed holiday. Most of ❸ our client companies are closed that day, and those that remain open are short-staffed. We receive many fewer phone calls and requests for services on that day. If it were changed to a floating holiday most employees would take the day off because they have long weekend plans; we would be keeping the office open for only a few employees.

My plan for making Presidents' day a floating holiday and keeping the day after Thanksgiving as a fixed holiday makes good sense. This plan would best serve the interests of our clients and our employees. ❺

❶ The first sentence clearly states the main idea of the memo.

❷ The final three sentences in the introductory paragraph provide a preview of the supporting details.

❸ Each paragraph focuses on developing one major point.

❹ Sometimes an additional supporting detail comes to mind as you write your first draft.

❺ The concluding paragraph summarizes the main idea and supporting details.

Revising and Editing

After you have finished your draft, read it to see that you have clearly stated and supported your main idea. Check for logical organization, transitions, and sentence structure variety. Revise your draft as necessary. Then go back and edit it for correct grammar, punctuation, spelling, and capitalization.

Model of Revised and Edited Draft

In response to your request for my input, I recomend *m* that we make Presidents' Day a floating holiday ~~and~~ *but* keep the day after Thanksgiving a fixed holiday. I base my opinion partly on the holiday policies of our client companies. I also considered how our employees feel about the issue. These policies and sentiments support treating the two holidays differently.

First of all, ❶ Changing Presidents' Day to a floating holiday makes sense. Most of our client companies conduct business on this day. Because we receive a typical number of phone calls and service requests, closing our office is *Second,* ❶ disruptive for our clients. Most of our employees state that their families do not have this day off. For this reason, they would prefer a floating holiday *their* ❷ to use when they can spend time with ~~there~~ families. Employees could also time their floating holiday to coincide with a school holiday, *So* finding child ❸ care on such a day would be unnecessary.

In contrast, The day after Thanksgiving should remain a fixed holiday. Most of our client companies are closed that day, and those that remain open are short-staffed. We receive many fewer phone calls and requests for services *In addition,* on that day. If it were changed to a floating holiday most employees would ❹ take the day off because they have long weekend plans; we would be keeping the office open for only a few employees.

My plan for making Presidents' *D*ay a floating holiday and keeping the *business* ❺ day after Thanksgiving as a fixed holiday makes good sense. This plan *both* would best serve the interests of our clients and our employees.

❶ Adding transitional words and phrases makes the organization of ideas clearer.

❷ In this context, the possessive pronoun *their* is the correct word to use.

❸ You can fix a fragment by combining it with another sentence.

❹ A comma should follow an introductory clause.

❺ Sometimes the addition of just one specific word helps make your point.

Presenting a Final Draft

After revising and editing, reread the final version of your writing before you submit the response or print it or e-mail it off to a coworker.

Model of Final Draft

In response to your request for my input, I recommend that we make Presidents' Day a floating holiday but keep the day after Thanksgiving a fixed holiday. I base my opinion partly on the holiday policies of our client companies. I also considered how our employees feel about the issue. These policies and sentiments support treating the two holidays differently.

Changing Presidents' Day to a floating holiday makes sense. First of all, most of our client companies conduct business on this day. Because we receive a typical number of phone calls and service requests, closing our office is disruptive for our clients. Second, most of our employees state that their families do not have this day off. For this reason, they would prefer a floating holiday to use when they can spend time with their families. Employees could also time their floating holiday to coincide with a school holiday, so finding child care on such a day would be unnecessary.

In contrast, the day after Thanksgiving should remain a fixed holiday. Most of our client companies are closed that day, and those that remain open are short-staffed. We receive many fewer phone calls and requests for services on that day. In addition, if it were changed to a floating holiday, most employees would take the day off because they have long weekend plans; we would be keeping the office open for only a few employees.

My plan for making Presidents' Day a floating holiday and keeping the day after Thanksgiving as a fixed holiday makes good business sense. This plan would best serve the interests of both our clients and our employees.

Testing Tip

When taking the Business Writing test on paper, you won't have time to copy your revised and edited version as a final draft. That is understood by the scorers and will not count against you if you have marked changes neatly.

KEY POINTS

When writing for business:

→ Prewrite to generate ideas, identify your main idea, and organize support.

→ Using your prewriting notes, write a first draft.

→ Revise your draft to improve organization, style and tone, and sentence structure.

→ Edit your draft, making corrections in grammar and mechanics as necessary.

Unit 1
Development of Ideas

Secondary school counselors confer with students and their parents about students' course selection, study skills, and career planning. They also help students identify their abilities, interests, and personality traits. As part of their jobs, secondary school counselors are required to do much writing. Among other writing responsibilities, they maintain student records and write letters of recommendation for students applying to colleges, universities, and places of business. The ability to develop ideas and express them in writing is crucial to their job success.

In your job, you may also be required to develop and elaborate ideas in memos, letters, or reports. To move forward with your career, you must have strong ideas and opinions and use well-chosen details to support them. Show your boss or coworkers exactly what you mean. The lessons in this unit will provide practice in these writing skills:

→ **Lesson 1** Conveying Your Main Idea
→ **Lesson 2** Supporting Your Main Idea
→ **Lesson 3** Giving Examples, Facts, and Reasons
→ **Lesson 4** Keeping to the Topic

To succeed at work, you must learn how to develop your ideas and express them in writing to show readers—your supervisor, coworkers, clients, or customers—why you think as you do. Mastering this skill will allow you to produce writing that resonates with others and that will set you apart as a valued employee.

Conveying Your
Main Idea

KEY *Words*

main idea a writer's main point; sometimes called the **controlling idea** or **central focus**

topic sentence a statement of the main idea near the beginning of a piece of writing

WorkKeys® in REAL LIFE

Receptionists greet visitors to a business and take phone calls. They also relay phone messages to their coworkers and supervisors in written notes or e-mails. They need to be sure they convey a message accurately. The main point of the caller's phone call must be clear in their writing.

Human resources assistants compile and keep records on employees. They explain company policies and prepare memos and other documents concerning employee activities. Each document a human resources assistant writes must contain a clear main idea so that employees can understand the main point of the document.

The Skill

Many jobs require some form of writing, and there are many forms of business writing—e-mails, letters, memos, notes, meeting records, messages, reports. Yet every business writer writes for one main reason—to get a point across.

The writer's main point is the **main idea**. When you prewrite, think clearly about what you want to say. What is the point you want your coworkers or boss to understand? When you begin to write, express that main idea in a **topic sentence** at the beginning of your writing. If you're stating your opinion, you don't need to begin your main idea with "I think" or "I believe."

Your topic sentence should be neither too general nor too specific. A topic sentence is too general when it states your topic but does not include the main point you want to make about that topic. A too-general topic sentence won't focus your coworkers' or boss's attention on your main point. On the other hand, avoid writing a topic sentence that is too specific—one that just states a detail about your topic. A too-specific topic sentence will not convey your main point to your coworkers or boss.

Your main idea, then, comes first in a clearly stated topic sentence. Follow it with details that support or explain your main idea.

HERE'S HOW

What's the Job? Receptionists are responsible for writing messages, along with other assigned duties. Read the message that a receptionist wrote for a coworker while she was away from her desk.

> One of your customers, Ms. Judy Hager, cannot make your 1:00 scheduled meeting with her today. She is running late because ❶ of a flat tire. She can meet you at 4:00 today if you have time. Please call her (555-894-1333) as soon as possible after you return to your desk.

❶ The topic sentence appears at the beginning of the message and clearly states the main idea.

A too-general topic sentence would be "A customer can't make your meeting." A too-specific topic sentence would be "Ms. Judy Hager had a flat tire." The receptionist wrote an effective topic sentence that stated the main point of the message.

Read the following details of a message from a man named Peter Epps. Then, choose the best topic sentence for it.

> He wants to know the cost of advertising on three screens for six months. He also asked whether the ads need to be paid in full or whether installments are acceptable. He specifically liked your third idea for an ad but wondered whether he could make a minor change.

Which of these statements would be the best topic sentence?

A. Peter Epps called about advertising.

B. Peter Epps is interested in buying advertising but needs more details.

C. Peter Epps liked your third idea for an ad.

What Do I Need to Know? Look carefully at the details.

- Ask yourself, what main idea do all three details add up to?
- The first topic sentence states the topic—Peter Epps's phone call. But it doesn't state what is important about the phone call. It is too general.
- The third topic sentence is just a detail from the message. It is too specific.
- The second topic sentence states the main point of the message. It's the best topic sentence.

Try It

Use a sheet of paper for these writing activities.

Activity 1 Write *OK* if the underlined topic sentence effectively tells the main idea of the message. If it is too general or too specific, write a new topic sentence.

1. <u>Our hospital would like to thank your company for its support of our recent blood drive.</u> The response of your employees was tremendous. Almost three-quarters of your workers donated blood. Because of their generosity, our blood supply should be sufficient for the coming several months.

2. <u>There is a safety problem.</u> When using the forklift on the floor, be sure you can clearly see ahead and to each side. Do not drive with your load raised. Be sure your light and sound signals are working so that customers and your fellow employees are aware that you are moving in the area. We recently had a near accident because these rules were not followed.

3. <u>We don't know how many tiles were burned.</u> Southwest Tile has notified us that they recently had a fire in one of their warehouses. They insist that orders will be delayed by no more than two weeks. However, before placing new orders with Southwest, please check other suppliers to see whether the product you need can be obtained from them.

What's the Job? Human resources assistants help write memos announcing company activities to the employees. The following memo was written by a human resources assistant.

Activity 2 Read the memo. Then, write a topic sentence for it.

> **ATTN: EMPLOYEES**
> The picnic will begin at 10:00 A.M. at Picnic Shelter B in the Lincoln Forest Preserve across from our building's main entrance. All employees' families are welcome, but you need to let me know by Thursday (Lupe Aragon, ext. 577) how many people from your family will be coming so that we know how much food to get. Last year, too many people came at the last minute, and we ran out of burgers and fruit. We don't want that to happen again this year. Thank you for your cooperation. We hope to see you all at the Employee Appreciation Picnic.

See page 112 for sample answers.

Your Turn

Use your own paper to write a response to the prompt on this page. When writing your response, remember to follow the writing process.

Prewrite: Generate and list your ideas about the topic. **Figure out what your main idea is.** Then, organize your ideas.

Draft: Write your draft using your ideas and your plan for organization. **Write your main idea in a topic sentence near the beginning of the draft.**

Revise: Read your draft, looking for ways to improve it. **Make sure your main idea is clearly stated.**

Edit: Read your draft again, looking for errors in grammar, spelling, capitalization, and punctuation.

Testing Tip

Read through the writing prompt slowly and carefully. Then, read it a second time, noting key words that tell you the topic (*allowing some employees to work from home*) and what to write (*a letter explaining whether you are in favor of it*).

Prompt:

At your company, some employees work mainly on computers and could perform their jobs at home. Other employees, however, must be physically present on company grounds to do their jobs. Management is considering allowing office workers with computers at home to telecommute, or work from home, three days a week.

Write a letter to the Human Resources department in your company explaining whether you are in favor of allowing some employees to telecommute.

KEY POINTS

When writing for business:

→ Think of your main point.

→ Write this main idea in a topic sentence at the beginning of your writing.

→ Follow your main idea with details that help explain or support it.

See page 112 for a sample response.

Supporting Your
Main Idea

KEYS TO...

Supporting Your Main Idea

When reading the lesson, keep the following points in mind:

→ Write your main idea in a topic sentence.

→ Add details that help explain and support the topic sentence.

→ Develop the main idea instead of repeating it.

WorkKeys® in REAL LIFE

Librarians perform a variety of tasks, including locating information, helping patrons, and developing library policies and procedures. They must be skilled communicators who convey clear messages to coworkers, supervisors, and library patrons. When they write, librarians must make sure they explain their message with supporting details.

Sales representatives contact new and existing customers, answer questions about products, and exchange tips with colleagues about selling strategies. Each document a sales representative writes must state and support a main idea so that others will understand the message.

The Skill

Each day, many workers and their bosses read memos and e-mails. They want messages that are concise, clear, and easy to read. In the fast-paced business world, the ability to write well is a skill that employers value and that gives workers a leg up.

Keep in mind the structure of the messages you write. A message has a beginning—which is a topic sentence—a middle, and an end. After you have stated your main idea in a topic sentence, you develop it; that is, you write sentences that give **supporting details** to explain and illustrate your main point.

Developing your main idea begins with prewriting. When you prewrite, list ideas that support your main point. You might ask yourself, "What does my coworker or my boss need to know to understand my point? What details give added, essential information?" For example, a sales rep might write to a customer, "We have some exciting new products that would do well for you and your store." To support that main idea, he might write, "Our new glossy paint is already a best-seller."

When you begin to write, put your ideas from prewriting into sentences. Each sentence that follows the topic sentence should state one of these well-chosen details.

KEY *Words*

supporting details specific details that explain or illustrate the topic sentence

HERE'S HOW

What's the Job? Librarians are responsible for writing memos and articles, along with performing other assigned duties. Read the article that a librarian wrote for a newsletter to patrons.

> *"At the Library"* is our cable television program about the Glenmore Public Library, produced in cooperation with the village of Glenmore. On this program, host Judy Andrews explores the events and happenings at the library. Each thirty-minute episode includes book reviews, interesting interviews, and monthly program highlights. The program airs each Tuesday at 8:00 P.M. on WON (channel 8). **❶**

Notice how the highlighted sentences support the topic sentence. The second sentence identifies the host and tells what she will do. The third sentence describes the content of each episode, and the fourth sentence tells when the program is shown. The librarian wrote an effective second sentence that helped to explain the main point.

Read the following topic sentence of an article.

> The Glenmore Public Library Foundation welcomes Joan Alexander, who will make an inspirational presentation.

Which of these sentences provides an additional detail that supports the main idea?

A. Library presentations are an enjoyable and educational way for patrons to spend their time.

B. The presentation is an uplifting account of the impact a few determined and caring individuals had on their neighborhood.

C. Award-winning authors usually are excellent speakers.

What Do I Need to Know?

- The first sentence makes a general statement about library presentations, not about Alexander's presentation.
- The third sentence makes a general statement about authors.
- The second sentence provides an additional detail that helps explain the main point of the message. It is an appropriate supporting detail to include with the main idea.

KEYS *to Success*

A common writer's mistake is to merely keep repeating the main idea. After writing a message, read it and ask yourself: *Does each sentence that follows the topic sentence tell something new and essential about the main idea?*

❶ Each sentence after the first contains a detail that supports the main idea by explaining something about the library cable television program.

Try It

Use a sheet of paper for these writing activities.

Activity 1
Read each topic sentence. Then, choose the sentences below it that contain supporting details. Write the topic sentence and supporting sentences as a paragraph.

1. A traveling exhibit, "Abraham Lincoln: the Self-Reliant Leader," will be on display at the Glenmore Public Library.
   a. The exhibit features artifacts from Lincoln's life—such as his high hat—and the Civil War.
   b. The exhibit runs from October 14 until November 6.
   c. This exhibit comes to Glenmore from Liberty Township Library.
   d. All are invited to tour it for free during the library's regular hours.

2. Intellectual freedom is the theme of Banned Books Week at the Glenmore Public Library.
   a. During the week the library will focus on the benefits of free access to information and the harm of censorship.
   b. The Constitution guarantees freedom of the press.
   c. The library will highlight books that have been the target of censorship.
   d. These books include *Huckleberry Finn* and *The Catcher in the Rye.*

What's the Job? Sales representatives often write memos to share selling tips with their colleagues. The following memo was written by a sales representative for a textbook publisher.

Activity 2 Read the memo. Then, write a second sentence for it that supports the main idea.

To: All Illinois Sales Reps
Re: Sales Tip

In selling our textbooks in my Illinois district, I have found that a new feature in the grade 11 literature book is grabbing attention. [2] Some of the authors included in this feature are Carl Sandburg, Gwendolyn Brooks, Vachel Lindsay, Nelson Algren, and Saul Bellow. Many teachers have a soft spot for local writers. Showing Illinois teachers this feature is a way to make a good opening impression and spark interest in our books. One or two teachers even commented that this feature sets our product apart from other publishers' books.

See pages 112–113 for sample answers.

Your Turn

Use your own paper to write a response to the prompt on this page. When writing your response, remember to follow the writing process.

Prewrite: Generate and list your ideas about the topic. Figure out what your main idea is. **Identify ideas that support and explain that main idea.** Then organize your ideas.

Draft: Write your draft using your ideas and your plan for organization. Write your main idea in a topic sentence near the beginning of the draft. **Write your supporting details in the sentences following your topic sentence.**

Revise: Read your draft, looking for ways to improve it. **Make sure that you have supported your main idea with details.**

Edit: Read your draft again, looking for errors in grammar, spelling, capitalization, and punctuation.

Testing Tip

On the Business Writing Test, review your writing to see if you have supported your main idea. You may think of another supporting detail to add. If you are writing online, insert it. If you are writing your response on paper, you can insert a caret where you want to place the detail and write it neatly in the margin.

Prompt:

A coworker wants you to sign a letter that asks for an across-the-board raise for all eight workers in your office. She believes that if all of you make this group request, you are more likely to get a favorable answer. Another coworker does not want to sign the letter. He thinks that each worker is different and that some may be worthy of a raise while others are not. Write a letter to your coworkers that states your opinion on this issue and what your reasons are.

KEY POINTS

When writing for business:

➜ Write your main idea in a topic sentence at the beginning of your writing.

➜ Follow the topic sentence with sentences that provide details that support it.

➜ Develop your main idea. Do not just repeat it; explain it.

See page 113 for a sample response.

Giving Examples, Facts, and Reasons

WorkKeys® in REAL LIFE

Employment interviewers speak directly to people who are applying for jobs in an organization. They must understand the demands of each job, and they must have excellent "people skills" in order to determine whether a candidate is right for a position. Summaries that an employment interviewer writes must contain specific information about a candidate's skills and experience.

Secondary school counselors support the academic, social, and emotional development of teenage students. They meet with students, teachers, and parents when challenges arise. They make recommendations for support services when necessary. School counselors' reports must provide relevant facts and details to support recommendations.

The Skill

In the last lesson, you learned about writing supporting sentences that provide more information about your main idea. What kinds of details support a main idea? Here are three types of sentences you can use to make your writing clearer to a reader.

An **example** is an idea you can add to actually show what you mean. If a topic sentence says that a job candidate was well-dressed, an employment interviewer might add a sentence briefly describing his appearance.

A relevant **fact** can be used to "prove" your main idea. For example, if the main idea is that a job candidate was late for her interview, the interviewer might consider adding a sentence that the appointment was scheduled for 9:00 A.M. but the person did not arrive until 9:25.

Finally, you need to support your main point with specific **reasons**, or explanations for it. A topic sentence such as "Marisol would be an excellent fit for this job" will not be convincing unless it is followed by reasons *why* she is a good fit. For example, an employment interviewer might highlight her previous job and how it matches the current job description.

KEY *Words*

example   a clear statement that illustrates a point

fact   a true statement. A relevant fact supports an opinion.

reason   an explanation for a point of view

HERE'S HOW

What's the Job? School counselors often write reports that recommend specific supports for struggling students. Read part of such a report below and notice the specific reason, example, and fact used to support the topic sentence.

> Because Carl is still catching up with schoolwork after the sudden death of a grandparent, I recommend that he be given extra time to complete his assignments. For example, Carl should be given until ❶ Friday to hand in his book report. He has read the entire book and written an introduction; he just needs time to write the rest of the report.

KEYS to Success

After writing your opinion in a recommendation or other piece, read it and ask yourself: *Have I provided sufficient examples, reasons, and facts to support my main point?* If not, add that information.

❶ In this report the main idea is stated in the last part of the first sentence. A reason precedes it; an example and a fact follow it.

First, the counselor gives a reason for her recommendation—Carl's grandparent died suddenly. Second, by offering a specific example of *how* a teacher can help Carl, the school counselor has made herself clearer. Finally, the counselor adds a fact to her memo. She states exactly where Carl is with his report; this information adds support to her main idea.

Read the following topic sentence from a memo sent by a school counselor. Then decide which supporting detail is an example, which is a reason, and which is a relevant fact.

> I am recommending that Gabriella receive an hour of counseling each week.

Which of these statements is an example? A reason? A relevant fact?

A. Gabriella is struggling with some personal issues.

B. She and I have made an appointment time of Thursday at noon.

C. Among other issues, her parents are going through a divorce.

What Do I Need to Know? Look carefully at the choices.

- Ask yourself: How does each detail help support the main idea, the recommendation?
- The first sentence (A) gives a reason for the topic sentence.
- The second sentence (B) provides a specific fact in support of the recommendation.
- The last sentence (C) describes one of the personal issues Gabriela is dealing with. It is an example.

Try It

Use a sheet of paper for these writing activities.

Activity 1 Identify one example, one fact, and one reason that support the topic sentence in each paragraph.

1. The break room has been a mess every afternoon for the past month, and we all need to do a better job keeping it clean. There were dirty dishes left on the table every day, and it is not the job of maintenance to clean up after us. We might want to set up a rotating cleaning schedule so that each of us is responsible for keeping the break room neat and clean. For example, I am willing to do it every other Monday, and each of you can choose a day every two weeks as well.

2. The most important quality in a customer service representative is a pleasant attitude. Regardless of how competent a representative is, if he or she treats a customer with disrespect or negativity, the customer is not being served well. For example, recently we had to fire a representative who spoke rudely to a customer on the telephone. Although this representative answered the customer's question accurately, his tone cost the company business, as the customer canceled an order.

What's the Job? Employment interviewers write summaries of job candidates and often recommend whom to hire. The following memo was written by an employment interviewer.

Activity 2 Read the memo. Then add an example, a fact, or a reason that supports the topic sentence.

> **Date:** 01/25/12
> **To:** Hiring Panel
> **Re:** Administrative Assistant Position
>
> Of all the candidates I have interviewed for the position of administrative assistant, Sophia Mullings would be the best person for the job. Sophia has the work ethic and the intelligence necessary to excel in this demanding and fast-paced position.

KEYS to Success

As you write, try beginning a sentence with the words "For example." This strategy usually helps writers add an example. Try beginning a sentence with "In fact" to come up with a relevant fact. Read your main point with the word *because* after it to help you think of reasons.

Your Turn

Use your own paper to write a response to the prompt on this page. When writing your response, remember to follow the writing process.

Prewrite: Generate and list your ideas about the topic. Figure out what your main idea is. Identify ideas that support and explain that main idea. **Try to add more details—examples, facts, and reasons.** Then organize your ideas.

Draft: Write your draft using your ideas and your plan for organization. Write your main idea in a topic sentence near the beginning of the draft. **Write your supporting details, including examples, facts, and reasons, in the sentences following your topic sentence.**

Revise: Read your draft, looking for ways to improve it. **Make sure that you have supported your main idea. If you can, add more examples, facts, and reasons.**

Edit: Read your draft again, looking for errors in grammar, spelling, capitalization, and punctuation.

Testing Tip

During prewriting, jot down ideas in response to the prompt; identify your main idea; then look at each supporting idea. Ask yourself, "What example can I give to explain this idea? What fact is relevant to it? What reason helps support it?"

Prompt:

The person you work for is trying to decide whether to hire a part-time person to help you get more work done. The alternative is to have you work an additional hour each day for more pay.

Write a letter to your supervisor explaining whether you are in favor of hiring an additional worker or working additional time yourself.

KEY POINTS

When writing for business:

➔ Support your main idea with details, including examples, facts, and reasons.

➔ Examples help the reader see what you mean.

➔ Relevant facts explain and make your writing clear.

➔ Reasons help persuade your reader.

See page 113 for a sample response.

Keeping to the
Topic

WorkKeys® in REAL LIFE

Nurse managers supervise the activities of nursing staff in a hospital or some other medical facility. They write reports and memos evaluating the performance of employees under their supervision. They also use reports, memos, and e-mails to communicate with their staff and with other departments in the organization. Nurse managers must focus on a clear topic in each document they write.

Building inspectors inspect structures to make sure that they are in good repair and in compliance with building codes. They write inspection reports, as well as violation notices and recommendations for bringing the building into compliance with the codes. Each document a building inspector writes should focus on the issue being addressed so that recipients can clearly understand the ideas being expressed in the document.

The Skill

Business writing includes many forms, such as e-mails, letters, memos, and reports. Although these written communications are different in form, each piece of good business writing is focused on one particular topic and the writer's main idea about that topic.

When you begin prewriting, think about your topic. For a building inspector, the topic could be the condition of a particular building. Begin jotting down your thoughts and identify your main idea, or what you want to say *about* that topic. The building inspector might note that a building is dangerously damaged. Then, express that main idea in a topic sentence.

All the ideas that follow your topic sentence should relate to your main idea. For example, a memo on a damaged building should *not* include a statement about the difficulty the inspector had in locating the building. Writing that wanders away from the main point is confusing, making it difficult for readers to understand the main idea.

Therefore, as you choose ideas to write about, select only those that help explain and support your main idea. As you write, try not to let your thoughts—and writing—wander. When you revise, you will have one last chance to delete any **extraneous detail** that is not focused on your topic.

KEY Words

extraneous detail an idea that is not focused on the topic

HERE'S HOW

What's the Job? One of the duties of a nurse manager is to write annual employee performance evaluations. Read the evaluation that a nurse manager wrote for one of her nurses.

> Overall, Michelle's performance this past year has been excellent. Her clinical knowledge is strong, and she is especially good at giving emotional support to patients and their families. Her patient charts are always up to date, and her communication with doctors and other staff is excellent. In emergencies, she willingly takes extra shifts. She also eagerly worked on the hospital's Toys for Tots campaign. In addition, Michelle takes constructive criticism well. When I advised her that she was relying too heavily on consulting the on-call doctors, she began making simple decisions about patient care independently.

❶ The topic sentence clearly states the topic—Michelle's performance for the past year.

❷ This detail is extraneous. It does not give supporting information about Michelle's job performance.

The sentences in this evaluation generally keep to the topic—Michelle's performance. The second highlighted sentence, however, does not. The nurse manger should delete it before submitting her evaluation.

Read the following topic sentence from an evaluation. Then choose the extraneous detail that should be deleted.

> Tim's performance is unsatisfactory in several categories. He is careless in administering medication. He is often late in reporting for his shift. I have heard that Tim is recently divorced.

Which of these statements should be deleted because it does not keep to the topic?

A. Tim is careless in administering medication.
B. Tim is often late reporting for his shift.
C. Tim is recently divorced.

What Do I Need to Know? Think about the topic in this sentence—Tim's performance.

- The first two details relate to his performance. They deal with clinical skill and punctuality.
- The third detail—Tim's divorce—may *affect* his performance, but it is not directly related to the topic. The answer is *C—Tim is recently divorced.*

Try It

Use a sheet of paper for these writing activities.

KEYS to Success

Keep your audience in mind when you write about a particular topic. Is this topic appropriate for coworkers? Employees? Supervisors?

Activity 1 Write the main idea of each passage. Then, write the sentence that DOES NOT keep to the topic by supporting that main idea.

1. The new work schedule has had a beneficial effect on employee performance. Those employees who have chosen to work from home have increased their productivity by 10 percent. Employees who have chosen flex-time have lowered their absentee rate. Most employees would like to have the option of working through lunch.

2. Customer complaints have increased over the past quarter ending in August. Many employees were on vacation during this past quarter. In June our complaint department handled an average of 50 calls per day. In August the number of complaints rose to an average of nearly 70 calls per day.

3. Our investigation determined that the five-car accident on Highway 30 had several causes. The driver of the first car apparently fell asleep at the wheel seconds before impact. The driver of the tractor-trailer directly behind attempted to swerve, sideswiping the car in the next lane, which caused the next three cars to crash. This time of year can be very treacherous on the highways.

What's the Job? Building inspectors write detailed reports about the condition of the buildings they have inspected. The following is a report written by a building inspector.

Activity 2 Read the following report. Then, rewrite the paragraph, removing any words, phrases, or sentences that do not keep to the topic.

INSPECTION REPORT
LOCATION: BUILDING AT 512 FRONT STREET
OVERVIEW

The home at 312 Front Street has several areas of damage caused by the recent hurricane. Unlike the hurricane of 2001, this hurricane was a direct hit on the city. The roof of this building was completely torn off by the high winds. Meteorologists report that winds reached 120 miles per hour. A tree in the front yard was uprooted, striking and destroying the front bay window. Windows are often destroyed by flying debris in a hurricane. Siding on the east side of the building was partially ripped off, and flying debris also damaged the garage door. Repairing this home will be costly.

Your Turn

Use your own paper to write a response to the prompt on this page. When writing your response, remember to follow the writing process.

Prewrite: Generate and list your ideas about the topic. Figure out what your main idea is. **Add details, but then choose only the details that support your main idea.** Organize your ideas.

Draft: Write your draft using your ideas and your plan for organization. Write the main idea about your topic in a sentence near the beginning of the draft. **Write supporting sentences that include only ideas that reinforce your main idea.**

Revise: Read your draft, looking for ways to improve it. **Make sure all ideas relate to the topic. Delete those that don't.**

Edit: Read your draft again, looking for errors in grammar, spelling, capitalization, and punctuation.

Testing Tip

Keeping to your plan and the ideas you chose to write about in prewriting is a good way to stay on topic. However, as you write, don't hesitate to add specific examples and other solid ideas that come to mind. Be sure, though, that they add support to your main idea and don't wander off topic.

Prompt:

The personnel manager in your company has decided to change the official work hours and require employees to come to work at 8:00 A.M. instead of 9:00 A.M. Employees would still work a regular 8-hour day. The personnel manager believes that people are more alert and productive early in the day, and he has noticed people leaving early at the end of the day anyway. Write a letter to the personnel manager explaining whether or not you are in favor of the earlier starting time. Give specific reasons for your point of view.

KEY POINTS

When writing for business:

→ Make sure that all ideas relate to the topic.

→ Include only ideas that support your main idea.

→ After you write, read your writing to see if any extraneous details should be deleted.

See page 114 for a sample response.

GOING FOR THE GOLD For the Unit 1 Assessment, go to www.mysteckvaughn.com/CAREER.

Unit 2
Organization

Computer support specialists set up equipment for their coworkers' use and monitor their company's computer systems. Although their work primarily entails troubleshooting and problem solving, they also write on the job. Computer support specialists keep detailed records of problems reported and solutions achieved. They may also write training materials to teach their fellow employees how to use new software. To write well at their workplace and succeed in communicating technical information, they must organize their ideas carefully.

In your job, too, you must organize ideas so your coworkers can follow them easily. Your e-mails, memos, letters, and reports must present your ideas in a clear, logical way. You must provide an easy-to-follow structure with a beginning, a middle, and an end. This organizational pattern helps you achieve your purpose and builds confidence in your readers—confidence in you to provide the information they need. The lessons in this unit will help you practice these writing skills:

→ **Lesson 5** Writing Paragraphs
→ **Lesson 6** Writing an Introduction
→ **Lesson 7** Writing a Conclusion
→ **Lesson 8** Organizing and Using Transitions

Clear organization in writing reflects clear thinking, and clear thinking is a valuable characteristic for an employee to have and demonstrate.

Writing
Paragraphs

KEYS TO...

Writing Paragraphs

When reading the lesson, keep the following points in mind:

→ A paragraph has three main parts.

→ The topic sentence expresses the main idea in the paragraph.

→ All details in the paragraph should support, explain, or develop the main idea in the topic sentence.

→ The last sentence restates or summarizes the main idea.

WorkKeys® in REAL LIFE

Correspondence coordinators prepare documents like damage claims, service complaints, and response letters. In all of these documents, paragraphs must contain a main idea and be well organized.

Computer support specialists oversee the performance of computer systems. They answer questions from computer users to resolve problems, and they develop training materials and procedures. Each document a computer support specialist writes must have concise paragraphs that contain a clear idea about a single topic so that employees can understand the information or instructions contained in the document.

KEY Words

supporting sentences the "body" of the paragraph. Supporting sentences follow the topic sentence and contain details to support, explain, or develop the topic.

closing sentence the last sentence in a paragraph. It restates or summarizes the main idea of the paragraph.

The Skill

Most business writing is written in paragraphs. Good business writing contains clear, concise paragraphs that convey information in a logical manner. Effective paragraphs have three parts: the topic sentence, the **supporting sentences**, and the **closing sentence**.

You've seen that the topic sentence is usually the first sentence of a paragraph and contains the main point or main idea of the paragraph. All sentences in the paragraph are related to the topic sentence.

Supporting sentences follow the topic sentence and form the body of the paragraph. They contain details that support, explain, or develop the main idea in the topic sentence. Supporting sentences should be organized in a logical way. For example, if a topic sentence states *I have discovered three minor flaws in this machine*, the first supporting sentence should contain information about the first flaw, and so on. Sentences may be organized by order of importance, from general to specific, or from specific to general.

The closing sentence is the last sentence in a paragraph. It restates the topic in different words or summarizes the main idea of the paragraph. For example, *These three flaws do not affect the operation of the machine* might be the closing sentence for the paragraph described above.

Often business writing consists of more than one paragraph. As you generate details about your main idea, and then examples, facts, and reasons as further support, you develop a paragraph about each supporting idea.

HERE'S HOW

What's the Job? One of the duties of correspondence coordinators is writing service complaint letters. Read the letter that a correspondence coordinator wrote to a heating/air conditioning company.

> Dear Mr. Harrison:
>
> Your recent service call to repair our air conditioner at this address has failed to correct the problem. The temperature throughout the building remains uneven. The front office is still much too warm. The file room at the back of the building is far too cold. Because your repair person failed ❶ to correct the problems, I am returning your invoice for services. ❷

❶ Each supporting sentence in the paragraph supports the main idea that the problem has not been solved. The body sentences follow a logical order: from general (uneven temperature throughout) to specific (hot in front, cold in back).

❷ The closing sentence restates the main idea in the topic sentence.

The paragraph follows the clear three-part format. Read just the topic sentence and the closing sentence; there's no explanation of how the repair failed. Read the paragraph without the closing sentence; the paragraph leaves the reader hanging.

Read the following details from a business letter. Then, choose the best closing sentence for this paragraph.

> Your letter of May 19 to Mr. Black will receive prompt attention. Although Mr. Black is out of town, I will forward this to him immediately. He has stated that he expects your letter and is eager to read and respond to it.

A. We sincerely hope he can get to this right away.
B. You can expect a reply from Mr. Black by tomorrow morning.
C. Mr. Black is currently on vacation but will be glad to hear from you.

What Do I Need to Know? Look carefully at the topic sentence. Ask yourself, what closing sentence best restates or summarizes it?

- The first closing sentence contradicts the idea that the letter will receive "prompt attention."
- The third sentence does not relate to the topic sentence.
- The second sentence emphasizes the main point of the paragraph. The answer is *B—You can expect a reply from Mr. Black by tomorrow morning.*

Try It

Use a sheet of paper for these writing activities.

KEYS to Success

After writing a paragraph on the job, read it and ask yourself: *Does this paragraph begin with a topic sentence that contains my main idea? Do the supporting sentences relate to the main idea? Does the closing sentence restate the topic sentence in different words or summarize the main idea of the paragraph?* If not, revise the paragraph to include these elements.

Activity 1 For each of the following paragraphs, identify whether the topic sentence, one of the supporting sentences, or the closing sentence needs revision. Then, write a revision for that sentence.

1. The main problem in this department is a lack of ongoing training for employees. Training has not kept up with changes in technology. Productivity suffers when employees have to struggle with new software they don't understand. Many of our employees are also new. These problems will continue until we establish ongoing training as a departmental policy.

2. We are happy to make an announcement. We have added the day after Thanksgiving and a personal day as official paid holidays. The personal day will be a floating holiday that employees can schedule at any time throughout the year. We hope that employees enjoy this change of holiday schedule.

3. I would like to request vacation time for December 16–23. My accumulated vacation time is more than 48 hours, so these six days will use most of that time. Since December 24 is a holiday, if these days are approved, I will return to work on Monday, December 27. I love the holidays and have lots of plans for this time.

What's the Job? Computer support specialists are responsible for writing employee training materials for company computer systems. The following paragraph was written by a computer support specialist as part of a training manual for new employees.

Activity 2 Read the paragraph. Then, revise the paragraph, placing supporting sentences in logical order. Add a concluding sentence.

> **STARTING UP THE SYSTEM**
>
> The following start-up procedure must be used to avoid any loss of data or damage to the system. You'll see that the power switch on the computer tower is located on the front panel. Press it firmly. It will turn red when pressed, indicating it is on. First, make sure that the light on the surge protector line is on. The machine will then boot up after a few seconds. As you're waiting, press the power light located on the monitor to turn it on. When the machine finishes booting, you will see a prompt to enter your password. Enter it. Your screen will then appear.

See page 114 for sample answers.

Your Turn

Use your own paper to write a response to the prompt on this page. When writing your response, remember to follow the writing process.

Prewrite: Generate and list your ideas about the topic. Figure out what your main idea is. Then, organize your ideas.

Draft: Write your draft using your ideas and your plan for organization. Write your topic sentence for your response. **Then write paragraphs supporting that main idea. For each paragraph, write a topic sentence. Organize supporting sentences in a logical manner. Write a closing sentence that restates or summarizes the main idea of the paragraph.**

Revise: Read your draft, looking for ways to improve it. **Make sure your paragraphs have topic sentences, supporting sentences, and closing sentences.**

Edit: Read your draft again, looking for errors in grammar, spelling, capitalization, and punctuation.

Testing Tip

Each important supporting idea you generate for your main idea can be turned into the main idea of its own paragraph in the body of your response. Supporting sentences for each body paragraph will contain the examples, facts, and reasons that explain the supporting idea. Organizing your response in this way will help ensure a high score.

Prompt:

An office supervisor believes that too many important memos are not being read and understood by your work group. The supervisor thinks that the main problem is the overuse of e-mail to communicate. He is proposing that workers provide a printed copy of any communication that is considered high priority. Write a letter to this supervisor that states your opinion on this proposal and give reasons for your point of view.

KEY POINTS

When writing for business:

→ Organize your ideas in one or more paragraphs.

→ Write your main idea in a topic sentence at the beginning of each paragraph.

→ Write your supporting sentences in a logical order.

→ Write a closing sentence that restates or sums up the main idea of the paragraph.

See page 114 for a sample response.

Writing an
Introduction

KEYS TO...

Writing an Introduction

When reading the lesson, keep the following points in mind:

→ The introduction begins with a broad statement leading to a main idea.

→ From the main idea, an introductory paragraph moves the reader into the body of the message.

WorkKeys® in REAL LIFE

Public relations managers are concerned with how the community perceives a particular business or organization. They respond to requests for information, prepare and edit publications, develop and maintain company Internet pages, and write press releases. They often prepare formal reports or long pieces of writing with catchy introductions.

Human resources recruiters interview applicants to obtain information about their work history and job skills, evaluate applicant qualifications, and inform potential applicants about career opportunities within an organization. They must be able to communicate effectively in writing to supervisors and peers. To do so, they must know how to create introductory paragraphs that stir interest in their ideas and opinions.

The Skill

Writing effective introductory paragraphs is a way to capture attention on the job. A solid introduction makes your longer documents and reports easier to understand and will help get your point across. You will come across as a careful, organized thinker.

The **introduction**, or the first paragraph of a document, has its own structure, different from the body paragraphs. You might visualize it as a funnel—wide at the top, narrowing to a straight channel. The structure reflects the purpose of this paragraph: namely, to introduce your topic by first catching the reader's interest in it, leading the reader to your main idea about it, and then channeling your reader into the body of your message by pinpointing what you will say about it.

For example, a public relations manager for a community orchestra might begin a promotional piece with a statement about the excellence of the orchestra, a topic sentence stating that this excellence can be heard during the upcoming season, and three reasons people should attend the orchestra's performances. These reasons are the supporting details of the main idea. Each is also the main idea of one of the body paragraphs of the release.

An introductory paragraph, then, starts wide and ends narrow, bringing your reader into the heart of your message.

KEY Words

introduction the beginning of a piece of writing that leads the reader to the heart of the writer's message

HERE'S HOW

What's the Job? Public relations managers are responsible for writing press releases. Read the introductory paragraph of a press release written by a public relations manager.

> For caring parents, it is never too early to begin saving for their children's college education. With education costs soaring each year, parents must ❶ set up an adequate savings plan to meet their children's future college expenses. Fortunately, your local bank, Premier Savings, is sensitive to the concerns of parents. It has begun a new program, Education +. Three ❷ features—ease of deposits, high interest earnings, and tax deferment—make Education + the way to save for future college costs.

❶ The first sentence of the introductory paragraph makes a broad statement about the subject: namely, the need to begin saving early for college education.

❷ Here is the statement of the main idea.

The final sentence lists three key features of the new program. They help explain the main idea. Each feature will also be explained in greater detail in one of the paragraphs that follow this introduction.

Read the following sentences from the introductory paragraph of a press release. Then, choose the best opening sentence.

> Companies that make products for children must share the concerns of parents. *My Angel* has always put children first. Our new line of baby food is made from natural ingredients only.

Which of these statements would be the best opening sentence?

A. Organic products are more healthful than nonorganic ones.
B. Baby food varies greatly in quality.
C. Parents are deeply concerned about the health of their children.

What Do I Need to Know? Look carefully at the three sentences.

- Choice A is a general statement, but it does not connect to the second sentence.
- Choice B is a general statement, but it does not lead the reader to the main point.
- Choice C is a general statement that connects to the second sentence and leads readers to the main point. The answer is *C—Parents are deeply concerned about the health of their children.*

Try It

Use a sheet of paper for these writing activities.

Activity 1 Read the following memo from a sales manager. Then, write an introductory paragraph around the topic sentence.

Topic sentence: Unfortunately, our company experienced a steep drop in sales (20 percent) of school products during the previous quarter.

Traditionally, the summer months are a slow period. Schools are not in session, and many teachers and administrators are not at the schools. This seasonal nature of our business traditionally accounts for at least a small decrease in sales.

A second factor is increased pressure from our competitors. One of our competitors, Sandford and Company, reported a slight increase in sales even during this slow period. That company pursued an aggressive promotional campaign throughout the summer months.

To stay competitive, our company must initiate new sales and marketing strategies for the summer months.

What's the Job? Human resources recruiters sometimes write reports to supervisors about issues that affect employee productivity. The following is a report prepared by a human resources recruiter.

Activity 2 Read the report. Then, write an introduction for it.

ATTN: ALL DEPARTMENT MANAGERS
RE: PRODUCTIVITY STUDY RESULTS

The study was conducted over a period of nine months. Each employee was evaluated and given a rating on four criteria: the quantity of work completed, interactions with others, level of morale, and proficiency at assigned tasks. Some employees worked alone to complete a task. Others worked in teams of three or more members. Some teams were assigned members; for other teams, employees were allowed to choose members.

The results of the study are conclusive. Employees who worked in teams— whether assigned or self-selected— were more productive than those who worked alone.

See page 114 for sample answers.

Your Turn

Use your own paper to write a response to the prompt on this page. When writing your response, remember to follow the writing process.

Prewrite: Generate and list your ideas about the topic. Figure out what your main idea is. Then, organize your ideas.

Draft: Write your draft using your ideas and your plan for organization. **Write your main idea in a topic sentence in an introductory paragraph.** Write body paragraphs for each of your important supporting ideas.

Revise: Read your draft, looking for ways to improve it. **Make sure your introductory paragraph leads the reader to the main idea.**

Edit: Read your draft again, looking for errors in grammar, spelling, capitalization, and punctuation.

Testing Tip

Some writers find it helpful to write the main idea of their response in a topic sentence, write their body paragraphs, and then return to the beginning to develop their main idea into an introductory paragraph.

Prompt:

After a disagreement in your organization, a human resources consultant was hired to help employees work together in a better way. After interviewing all workers, she explained what she believed the problem was. Some people thought of their co-workers simply as fellow employees—individual people who worked for the same organization. Other employees thought of their co-workers as part of their "team"—colleagues who helped one another work toward a common goal. The consultant believed that the organization needed to decide on an "individual" style or a "team" style of working together. Write a letter to the head of your organization explaining which approach you think would be best, and give reasons why.

KEY POINTS

When writing for business:

➜ Keep in mind the structure of the introductory paragraph.

➜ Begin the introductory paragraph with a broad statement about your topic.

➜ Write your main idea in a topic sentence.

➜ Tell your reader what important points you will make about that main idea.

See page 115 for a sample response.

Writing a
Conclusion

KEY Words

conclusion   the ending or final paragraph of a long document or report

WorkKeys® in REAL LIFE

Product promoters demonstrate and explain products, set up and arrange displays, and report product-related information. They sometimes write reports to supervisors and co-workers. To get their ideas accepted, they must know how to write effective conclusions.

Loan counselors interview applicants and request information for loan applications, refer loans to loan committees, and sometimes even approve loans themselves. They must be able to communicate well in writing to clients, supervisors, and committees. By writing effective conclusions, they can persuade their readers to adopt their views.

The Skill

A longer business document that needs an introduction and body paragraphs also requires a concluding paragraph.

The structure of this **conclusion** is opposite that of the introduction. As you have learned, an introductory paragraph begins with a broad statement, narrows to a specific main idea, and pinpoints what will be said about that main idea. A concluding paragraph, in contrast, begins with the main idea and a summary of the key points, and then widens to a final, broad statement. The structure of the concluding paragraph, then, is like that of a funnel turned upside down.

For example, a public relations manager for a community orchestra might write a piece enticing people to buy season tickets to the symphony's upcoming season. She supports that main idea by citing how the tickets are affordable, the music is enjoyable, and the concerts are even educational. She might write the following concluding paragraph:

"This season's performances of your community symphony will be affordable, enjoyable, and educational. Your season ticket purchase will reward you with night after night of musical excellence."

To write an effective concluding paragraph, then, start narrow and end wide. Restate the main idea in a summary statement of the key points, and then leave your reader with a final, general thought that helps sell your point.

HERE'S HOW

What's the Job? Product promoters write reports about product demonstrations. Read the concluding paragraph that a product promoter wrote to her supervisor.

> The cutouts of superheroes in action, therefore, enhanced the demonstration of our line of energy bars at Alpha Food Store, as evidenced by the greater percentage of customers that flocked to this display than to the one presented last month and by the increase in sales that resulted. Customers probably identified with the larger-than-life heroes, whom they admire and wish to emulate. Hero worship runs deep in the American spirit.

❶ The first sentence of a concluding paragraph restates the main idea of the writer.

❷ These details are the support explained in the body of the report.

The product promoter wrote an effective concluding paragraph. It restates her main idea, echoes her main points, and leaves the reader with a final, broad statement.

Read the following opening sentence from a concluding paragraph written by a product promoter. It restates his main idea.

> Our display, therefore, needs more pizzazz to catch the eye of potential customers.

Which of these statements would be the best final sentence for the concluding paragraph?

A. Customers' buying habits are constantly changing.

B. If sales do not increase this quarter, our company must consider drastic measures.

C. People tend to gravitate to the dazzling.

What Do I Need to Know? Look carefully at the sentences. Ask yourself, which one relates best to the main idea?

- Choice A makes a broad statement about customers but does not connect closely enough to the main idea.
- Choice B makes a statement that is not related to the main idea.
- Choice C makes a broad statement about what attracts customers and expresses a final thought related to the main idea. The answer is *C—People tend to gravitate to the dazzling.*

······ Try It ······

See page 115 for sample answers.

Use a sheet of paper for these writing activities.

Activity 1 Read the following memo. Then, follow the directions to write an effective conclusion for it. Write your choices as a concluding paragraph.

> Regarding the recent company proposal to allow telecommuting, employees should be allowed to work at home one day each week. There are two good reasons to make this policy change.
>
> First, employees would have more time to give to their work if they did not have to spend precious hours just getting to and from the office. As a result, their productivity would increase.
>
> Second, in the quiet of their homes, they could concentrate better on their assigned tasks. This atmosphere makes for a more stress-free environment.

1. Which would be a good restatement of the main idea and key points?
   a. Allowing telecommuting, then, would result in increased productivity due to saved time and less stress.
   b. Changing the company policy, then, would mean that employees could work at home.

2. Which would be a good closing sentence?
   a. Telecommuting is a policy that benefits employees and management.
   b. Some people, however, may abuse the privilege of telecommuting.

What's the Job? Loan counselors sometimes write formal letters of approval to loan committees. A loan counselor wrote the following letter.

Activity 2 Read the letter to the loan committee. Then, write a concluding paragraph for it.

> **To:** Loan Committee
> **Re:** Rogers Mortgage Loan
>
> After careful review of the financial and credit background of Mr. and Mrs. Eric Rogers, I feel the couple qualifies for a fifteen-year mortgage of $205,000.00 at 4.8% interest.
>
> Mr. and Mrs. Rogers are both productive employees with outstanding work histories. In addition, each has strong career potential.
>
> Both are good credit risks. Each has an excellent credit score. Balances on accounts are kept low and paid on time.
>
> They have no outstanding large debts to repay. In all likelihood, they will be able to make each monthly payment and repay this loan on time.

KEYS to Success

Before writing a concluding paragraph, go back and pick up key words or phrases that identify your major supporting details to echo in your conclusion.

Your Turn

Use your own paper to write a response to the prompt on this page. When writing your response, remember to follow the writing process.

Prewrite   Generate and list your ideas about the topic. Figure out what your main idea is. Then, organize your ideas.

Draft   Write your draft using your ideas and your plan for organization. Write your main idea in a topic sentence near the beginning of the draft. Develop your support in body paragraphs. Write an introduction. **Finally, write a concluding paragraph.**

Revise   Read your draft, looking for ways to improve it. **Make sure your conclusion restates your main idea.**

Edit   Read your draft again, looking for errors in grammar, spelling, capitalization, and punctuation.

Testing Tip

To write an effective conclusion in a timed writing test, restate your main position, repeat key words from the middle paragraphs, and provide a final statement that gives a broad perspective.

Prompt:

The human resources department in your organization is writing its policy recommendations regarding personal relationships in the workplace. Should employees be free to see each other socially outside the workplace? Can employees date one another if they remain professional at the office? What if two workers decide to get married? Write a memo that summarizes your point of view on these workplace issues and provide support for your ideas.

KEY POINTS

When writing for business:

→ Restate your main idea in the first sentence of the concluding paragraph.

→ Echo or suggest the key points you made in the middle section.

→ End the concluding paragraph with a broad statement that provides a final, related thought.

See page 115 for a sample response.

Organizing and Using Transitions

KEYS TO...

Organizing and Using Transitions

When reading the lesson, keep the following points in mind:

→ Paragraphs should be organized in a logical order. The type of organization should be appropriate to your topic.

→ Transitions should guide readers through a piece of business writing and be appropriate to the pattern of organization.

WorkKeys® in REAL LIFE

Business managers plan and coordinate supportive services of an organization. One of their duties is preparing operational reports that contain vital information for the operation of a company. The ideas in reports must flow in a logical, understandable manner. Appropriate organization and clear transitions help achieve this.

Technical writers write documents like equipment manuals and operating and maintenance instructions. To clearly convey instructions, paragraphs in these documents must be organized in a logical manner. Once the paragraphs are put in order, transitions signal logical connections between ideas. Clear organization and transitions help make technical documents more understandable.

The Skill

Paragraphs in a document can be organized in several ways, depending upon the subject matter. A few types of organization are common in business writing. In **emphatic order**, the ideas are arranged in order of importance. Persuasive writing often employs this type of organization. **Chronological order** arranges ideas in a time sequence. Reports explaining the failure of a system might use chronological organization, or they might use **cause and effect** organization, which presents events and what results from them. Some documents may show more than one type of organization. For example, emphatic order may contain some elements of cause and effect.

Each type of organization relies on particular transitions. Here are some examples:

- Emphatic order: *most important, less critical*
- Chronological: *first, second, then, next, after, before*
- Cause/effect: *because, therefore, so, consequently*

Transitions signal the relationship between ideas. "Then" signals another event in a sequence. "Because" signals that what follows is a cause of something stated previously. Words, phrases, clauses, even whole sentences can serve as transitions. Transitions are essential in making the ideas in your writing clear to your readers.

KEY Words

emphatic order   ideas arranged in order of importance

chronological order   ideas arranged in a time sequence

cause and effect   ideas arranged in the order of causes and their effects

transitions   words, phrases, or sentences that provide logical connections between ideas in a document

HERE'S HOW

What's the Job? Business managers are responsible for identifying business problems and suggesting solutions. Read the following excerpt from a memo explaining a new procedure.

> We can cut costs by revising our billing procedure. Currently our billing procedure requires three steps. First, the shipping clerk fills out form S-21 listing the items shipped. Then, the form is passed on to pricing clerks, who price each item. Finally, the priced order is passed on to an ❶ invoicing clerk, who prepares the invoice.
>
> These three steps can be streamlined to cut operational costs. First, we ❷ can provide the shipping clerk with access to the prices of all items. The clerk can enter the price on the order as it is filled. Once the items are shipped, this form can then be passed on to the invoicing clerk. This ❸ change eliminates step two in the process, thereby cutting costs. ❹

❶ These three transition words alert the reader to a sequence of events.

❷ This transitional sentence refers back to the three steps in the first paragraph, showing a logical progression of ideas and smoothly linking the two paragraphs.

❸ These three transition words once again signal a sequence.

❹ Even though the overall organization of these paragraphs is in chronological order, a transition showing a cause/effect relationship is appropriate to this sentence.

The business manager made the relationship between ideas clear by using appropriate transitions.

Read this excerpt from a business report. Then, choose the best set of transitions to complete the paragraph.

> Three problems persist. ___ problem is cost overruns. This is the most costly. ___ late delivery of product. ___ shipping costs have risen. This problem is most easily solved.

A. The most important; Finally is; Therefore, the problem
B. The least important; After that is; On the other hand
C. The most important; The next most costly is; Finally,

What Do I Need to Know? Look carefully at each sentence in the paragraph. Identify the overall organization. Items are listed in order of importance. The organization is emphatic order.

- In answer A "Finally" is in the second sentence. It belongs in the last.
- Answer B includes "On the other hand," a sign of contrast.
- In Answer C "most" and "next most" signal emphatic order. The answer is *C—The most important; The next most costly is; Finally.*

Try It

Use a sheet of paper for these writing activities.

Activity 1 Rewrite the following report, adding transitional words, phrases, or sentences where needed.

On Monday, January 12, we will institute our new staffing plan. ___ current employees will be organized into two teams. Team One will be responsible for handling and recording incoming calls and resolving them, if possible. ___ some complaints require research and background information before they can be resolved. Any complaints not handled by Team One will be forwarded to Team Two for research and resolution.

___, I anticipate we may have some problems. Not all employees will be acquainted with members of their new team. ___ older employees may resist change. ___ long-term employees may resent having new employees as supervisors.

___ The two team supervisors, Lucinda Young and Leon Cotton, are able supervisors. They have experience in integrating new team members and training staff in new procedures. ___ regular training seminars and weekly staff meetings should alleviate most of these problems.

What's the Job? Technical writers write instruction manuals for using technical equipment. The following paragraphs are from a user manual for a digital camera.

Activity 2 Read the paragraphs from the manual. Then, write a paragraph explaining how these paragraphs use transitions to help the ideas flow smoothly.

CHOOSING PRINT SIZE

To choose the print size for your image, first select the length of the long side. Then, select the length of the short side. See the table on page 16 for the available combinations of long side and short side lengths. Then press the OK button.

You may now trim the image to a specific print area. The trimming frame is different depending on the size of the print you have chosen. The trimming screen is also different in different camera models. Therefore, follow the instructions on the screen display on your camera.

See page 115 for sample answers.

Your Turn

Use your own paper to write a response to the prompt on this page. When writing your response, remember to follow the writing process.

Prewrite Generate and list your ideas about the topic. **Figure out what type of organization best suits your subject.**

Draft Write your draft using your ideas and your plan for organization. **Make sure you use appropriate transitions.**

Revise Read your draft, looking for ways to improve it. **Check to see that ideas and paragraphs follow one another smoothly. If not, review your transitions.**

Edit Read your draft again, looking for errors in grammar, spelling, capitalization, and punctuation.

Testing Tip

As you read through the writing prompt, look for clues that tell you how to organize your writing and what types of transitions you should use. For example, if you are told to give your reasons for an opinion, you should probably use emphatic order and transitions such as *The best reason.*

Prompt:

Your supervisor has recommended you for a different position within the company you work for. She has told you that this is not a promotion, nor is the salary higher. Instead, you would have the opportunity to see another department and get new experience. You have just gotten to the point in your current position where you feel confident and stress-free. You are curious about other departments, yet you also enjoy the job you are currently doing. Write a letter telling your supervisor whether you will take the new position or prefer to stay in your current role. Be sure to give reasons for your decision.

KEY POINTS

When writing for business:

→ Plan your pattern of organization before you begin writing.

→ Make sure each paragraph logically follows the previous one.

→ Use transitions within paragraphs and between paragraphs to link together ideas and make the ideas flow smoothly.

See page 116 for a sample response.

GOING FOR THE GOLD For the Unit 2 Assessment, go to www.mysteckvaughn.com/CAREER.

Unit 3
Style and Tone

Executive secretaries perform a variety of tasks throughout their busy day. Many of these tasks involve skillful writing. As part of their jobs, they draft memos, e-mails, invoices, and letters. They record the minutes at department meetings. They also conduct research and prepare reports read by committees and even boards of directors. To succeed at their jobs, executive secretaries must develop an effective writing style—one that is clear and concise, grammatically correct, and above all, professional in tone.

Like an executive secretary, you too may find the need to write clearly, concisely, and professionally to be successful at your job. Your writing should be clear and easy to read. It should sound like you—a professional—on paper. It must appear natural, graceful, and honest: a direct message from one worker to another, not a computer-generated printout. You want your words to be vivid, concrete, and precise; each word must count. Your style and tone should be professional, positive, and courteous. The lessons in this unit will help you practice these writing skills:

→ **Lesson 9** Using Standard Business English
→ **Lesson 10** Choosing Precise Words

Remember that a written message reflects its writer's personality and professional expertise. Your style and tone should convey the impression you want. Your writing stands for you.

Using Standard
Business English

KEYS TO...

Using Standard Business English

When reading the lesson, keep the following points in mind:

→ Use correct, grammatical English.

→ Use a professional, courteous tone.

→ Write clearly and directly.

WorkKeys® in REAL LIFE

Executive secretaries answer phone calls for their boss, handle general office duties, and attend meetings to record minutes. In their reports, memos, letters, financial statements, and other documents, they must be able to use standard business English effectively.

Advertising managers gather and organize information to plan advertising campaigns. They prepare advertising and promotional material to increase sales of products or services. To convey ideas and opinions clearly and convincingly, they must use standard business English.

The Skill

With friends and family, people use conversational English. Slang and other informal language are acceptable. With coworkers, clients, and bosses, however, **standard business English** is essential. In e-mails, memos, reports, and other business writing, workers who want to convey their message effectively and professionally use a certain kind of language.

Standard business English is grammatically correct English. Because it follows traditional usage and conventions, readers are better able to read and understand it. For example, "We will meet tomorrow morning" is clearer than "Gonna be meetin in the morning."

In addition, standard business English helps create a professional tone. **Tone** reveals the writer's attitude toward the subject or toward readers. By avoiding slang and buzzwords when you write, you sound like a serious employee. By avoiding rude language and highly charged words, even when your main idea is negative, you sound courteous and respectful.

Standard business English also involves a clear, direct style. No unnecessary words or phrases bog a reader down. No overly high-level words make the writing sound pompous or fussy. Whenever possible, the active voice moves the action along. For example, compare "Our team prepares the daily report" with "The daily report is prepared by our team."

To use standard business English effectively, follow the rules and conventions of English and choose words that convey your message professionally, courteously, clearly, and directly.

KEY Words

standard business English the type of writing required for business documents. It is grammatically correct and professional.

tone the writer's attitude toward the subject or readers

HERE'S HOW

What's the Job? Executive secretaries write many documents, including memos, letters, and reports. Read the following e-mail that an executive secretary wrote to members of her department.

> Our department will hold its monthly meeting this Wednesday, March 2, from 2:00 P.M. to 4:00 P.M. in the Wellington Room. Our guest speaker ❶ will be Sue Lyons, formerly a tennis pro and now a personal coach. Ms. Lyons will discuss ways to project a winning attitude when relating to coworkers, clients, and customers. Her presentation will entertain, inform, and inspire all of us.

❶ In this first sentence, as in the rest of the paragraph, the writer used correct grammar and followed conventions. She also used the active voice by writing "Our department will hold its monthly meeting," not "Our monthly meeting will be held. . . ."

The executive secretary wrote a message that is clear and direct and that conveys a professional tone.

Read the following sentences from different memos. Which one is the best example of standard business English?

A. The details of the sales report were discussed by every member of the committee.

B. Anyone with half a brain can tell that that proposal stinks.

C. At this point in time, our customers are indubitably laboring under the delusion that an increase in prices is well beyond a possibility.

D. Our department budget shows a slight increase in expenses for the third quarter.

E. All the dudes in the warehouse needs to fill out these forms.

What Do I Need to Know? Look carefully at each sentence. Ask yourself if it reflects all the elements of standard business English.

- Choice A does not use the active voice, which would be "Every member of the committee discussed the details of the sales report."
- Choice B uses rude language and creates a tone that is offensive, not professional.
- Choice C is not clear and direct. It uses unnecessary phrases and formal words that sound pompous and unnatural.
- Choice E has both slang (*dudes*) and a grammar mistake (*needs*).
- Choice D is grammatically correct, is clearly written, and has a professional tone. The answer is *D—Our department budget shows a slight increase in expenses for the third quarter.*

Try It

Use a sheet of paper for these writing activities.

Activity 1 Write *OK* if the sentence follows the rules of standard business English. If it does not, rewrite it so that it does.

1. An increase in prices for new uniforms gotta be implemented next month.

2. There is a violation of the dress code caused by employees who wear blue jeans to work.

3. Our department should hire an experienced writer to edit and revise company letters to clients.

4. Your claim that your training service creates positive learning experiences for new employees is a bunch of nonsense.

5. Because of the super tight schedule and real rigid deadlines for completing the project during the next two months, employees will no longer be having the privilege of telecommuting one day each week.

What's the Job? Advertising managers write memos to share promotional ideas with their team members. An advertising manager wrote the following memo to her team.

Activity 2 Read the memo. Then, identify the sentences that need revising to use standard business English. Explain what is wrong with each sentence and then rewrite it.

> Our new ad for the Roosevelt Theater shows promise. It has some strong features that will bowl over our client. For example, the image of a large red teardrop is gripping. It conveys both grief and horror and suits the classical tragedies listed in the left column. I also like the cool pictures of the playwrights running across the bottom border. They create a personal touch and send a clear message—namely, that real people wrote these plays. The ad, however, still needs something else to motivate theatergoers to buy tickets. The image of the laughing clown holding his sides is as old as the hills and makes me cringe. We need a fresh image to stand for comedy.

See page 116 for sample answers.

Your Turn

Use your own paper to write a response to the prompt on this page. When writing your response, remember to follow the writing process.

Prewrite: Generate and list your ideas about the topic. Figure out what your main idea is. Then, organize your ideas.

Draft: Write your draft using your ideas and your plan for organization. Write your main idea in a topic sentence near the beginning of the draft.

Revise: Read your draft, looking for ways to improve it. **Make sure you have used standard business English to create a professional tone.**

Edit: Read your draft again, looking for errors in grammar, spelling, capitalization, and punctuation.

Testing Tip

When revising and editing your response to the prompt, read it silently to yourself, but say each word in your head, as if you were speaking it aloud. That way, you can hear how the language sounds and the tone of the writing.

Prompt:

You are part of a working group at your company that gathers once a week to discuss trends in the industry. The group is trying to decide whether to pay an administrative assistant to take notes at your meeting or rotate the assignment among group members. The group would have to pay the assistant out of your own paychecks, but everyone would be able to focus on the discussion without worrying about notes. Alternatively, one group member would take notes each week and perhaps would be distracted by the task. Write a memo to your group stating which of these two plans you prefer and why.

KEY POINTS

When writing for business:
- → Use standard business English by following the rules of grammar.
- → Use a professional tone by avoiding slang and rude language.
- → Write clearly and directly.
- → Use the active voice.

See page 116 for a sample response.

KEYS TO...

Choosing Precise Words

When reading the lesson, keep the following points in mind:

→ Building word power will help you become a better writer.

→ Choose words that create clear pictures for your reader.

→ Use specific rather than general words to convey exact shades of meaning.

Choosing
Precise Words

WorkKeys® in REAL LIFE

Child, family, and school social workers counsel individuals, groups, and families. Social workers also keep detailed case histories of their clients and prepare reports, recommendations, and other documents. In their writing, they use precise words to convey their intended meaning.

Curators care for the items in a museum's collection. They plan exhibitions and conduct tours, workshops, and educational sessions to teach individuals about an institution's resources. Curators must use precise words to communicate effectively to the public and to fellow workers in writing.

The Skill

Good business writing is specific. It doesn't force readers to waste time wandering through generalities. As a business writer, make sure your **diction**, or word choice, is precise. Precise words paint clear pictures for your coworkers or boss. In that way they help convey your message and strengthen the impact of your writing.

Replace general or overused words—words that give almost no information—with precise and vivid words. For example, one supervisor wrote, "The committee did a good job in writing a nice report" and then revised her sentence to say, "The committee prepared an intriguing report." The second sentence avoids the general word *good* and replaces *did* and *nice* with precise words. *Nice* and *intriguing* both have positive associations, but *intriguing* tells so much more about why the report is positive—because it interests and stimulates one's thinking.

To improve your writing, replace general words with words that convey a specific meaning. For example—

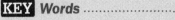

KEY Words

diction   word choice

General Words	Specific Words
needed	vital, essential
right	accurate, appropriate
nice, good	beneficial, effective
lots of	many, numerous

HERE'S HOW

What's the Job? School social workers are responsible for writing case histories, reports, and recommendations. Read the recommendation that a school social worker wrote to the school administration.

> Several freshmen whom I have interviewed seem self-conscious, withdrawn, and bewildered. At times, they find school ❶ overwhelming, with changing teachers, demanding courses, and unfamiliar faces in the hallways. Some freshmen do not concentrate well in class. Others do not know how to complete long assignments. Still others fear that bullies will torment them.
>
> Two initiatives would benefit these freshmen. First, require a course in basic study skills. Second, pair seniors with freshmen in a "buddy system." The seniors would offer a friendly smile as well as advice and support. Freshmen would appreciate mentors who can boost their confidence and teach them how to succeed in school.

❶ In the first sentence, the writer uses the specific words *self-conscious,* *withdrawn,* and *bewildered.* What other specific words do you notice in this paragraph?

The social worker chose specific words, such as *overwhelming,* *concentrate,* and *benefit* to convey her meaning. She avoided general words, such as *right, good,* and *nice.*

Read the following pairs of sentences from office memos. In each pair, identify the sentence that contains more specific words.
  A. Please think about the employees' ideas.
  B. Please analyze the employees' proposals.

  C. We need new marketing strategies to get good results.
  D. Innovative marketing strategies will spur sales.

What Do I Need to Know? Look carefully at the pairs of sentences.
- Ask yourself, which sentence uses more specific words?
- The first sentence in each pair uses general words: Choice A uses *think about* and *ideas;* Choice C uses *need, new, get,* and *good.*
- The second sentence in each pair uses more specific words: Choice B uses *analyze* and *proposals;* Choice D uses *innovative* and *spur.*
- The answers are *B* and *D—Please analyze the employees' proposals. Innovative marketing strategies will spur sales.*

KEYS *to Success*

Build your vocabulary so that you can choose precise words to transmit exact shades of meaning. Use a dictionary to learn new words and check definitions. Study a word's denotation (literal definition) as well as its connotations (positive or negative associations).

Try It

Use a sheet of paper for these writing activities.

Activity 1 Rewrite each sentence replacing general words with specific ones.

1. The items in the museum are important.

2. People think that parties after work are great.

3. New employees need to know about the good things our company offers.

4. Someone here should look at our competitors' new products.

5. It was not right for her to be passed over for promotion.

What's the Job? Curators help write memos, reports, and articles about the items in a museum's collection. A curator wrote the following memo to a junior curator on her staff.

Activity 2 Read the memo. Then identify the sentences that contain general words and rewrite them using specific words.

> **ATTN:** Bill Drake, Associate Curator
> **RE:** New Exhibit
>
> Our new exhibit, *The Age of Elizabeth*, will open in January of next year. It will show many of the early printed books and rare artifacts in our collection. The exhibit will especially be liked by teachers and students of British history and literature. It will allow them to look at letters in Queen Elizabeth's own handwriting and to see first editions of several of Shakespeare's plays as well as those of his contemporaries. To start the exhibit off right, I would like you to give a talk that will be an overview for our first-night audience.

See page 116 for sample answers.

Your Turn

Use your own paper to write a response to the prompt on this page. When writing your response, remember to follow the writing process.

Prewrite: Generate and list your ideas about the topic. Figure out what your main idea is. Then organize your ideas.

Draft: Write your draft using your ideas and your plan for organization. Write your main idea in a topic sentence near the beginning of the draft.

Revise: Read your draft, looking for ways to improve it. **Check your diction to make sure you have used specific and clear language.**

Edit: Read your draft again, looking for errors in grammar, spelling, capitalization, and punctuation.

Testing Tip

When revising your writing, read it silently and imagine how the words you have chosen sound. Remember that well-chosen, precise verbs will enliven your style.

Prompt:

The company you work for has announced a new goal of having all of its employees be proficient business writers. While many workers support this idea, they believe that in order to meet the goal, the company should offer on-site writing classes during lunch hour and after work. Company executives point out that there are free and low-cost classes held in the evenings all around the city and that workers should take advantage of these.

Write a letter to your department head explaining how you feel about this issue. Be sure to provide specific reasons and examples for your point of view.

KEY POINTS

When writing for business:

→ Choose specific words rather than overused, general ones.

→ Use words that create sharp pictures for your reader.

See page 117 for a sample response.

GOING FOR THE GOLD For the Unit 3 Assessment, go to www.mysteckvaughn.com/CAREER.

Choosing Precise Words **53**

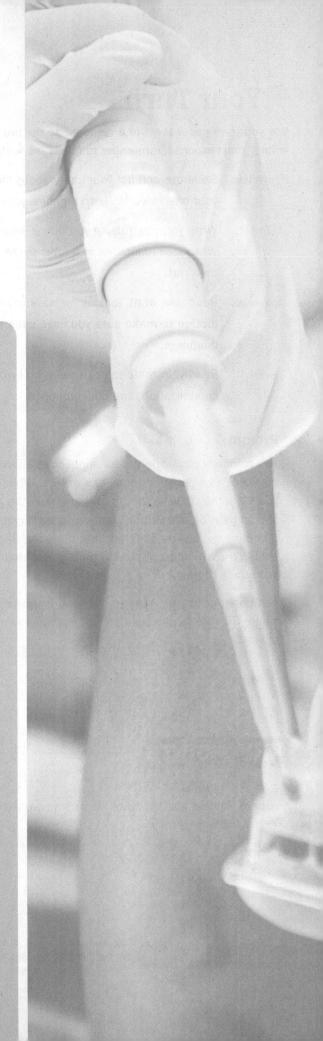

Unit 4
Sentence Structure

Laboratory technicians are skilled in chemical analysis. As part of their job, they examine cells, conduct blood tests, perform blood counts, and collect tissue samples. They also do much paperwork. For example, they send memos and reports to pathologists and record test data. To write well on the job, they must use sentences effectively to create informative and interesting writing.

Sentences are the building blocks of effective writing. In your job, if you need to write, you need to write effective sentences. Understanding sentence structure will help you express your ideas with greater precision. Combining, pulling apart, and reshaping sentences are part of the art of writing.

In this unit you will learn how to use compound sentences to coordinate ideas and complex sentences to subordinate one idea to another. Varying sentence structure will make your writing interesting, pleasing to read, and easy to read. In addition, you can make the information you convey flow smoothly from sentence to sentence. The lessons in this unit will provide practice in these writing skills:

→ **Lesson 11** Writing Complete Sentences

→ **Lesson 12** Using Compound Sentences

→ **Lesson 13** Using Complex Sentences

→ **Lesson 14** Achieving Sentence Variety

To write effectively on the job, you must construct sentences thoughtfully and creatively and link them clearly. Well-constructed sentences are a pleasure to read. They hold your coworker's or boss's interest and show a careful thinker at work.

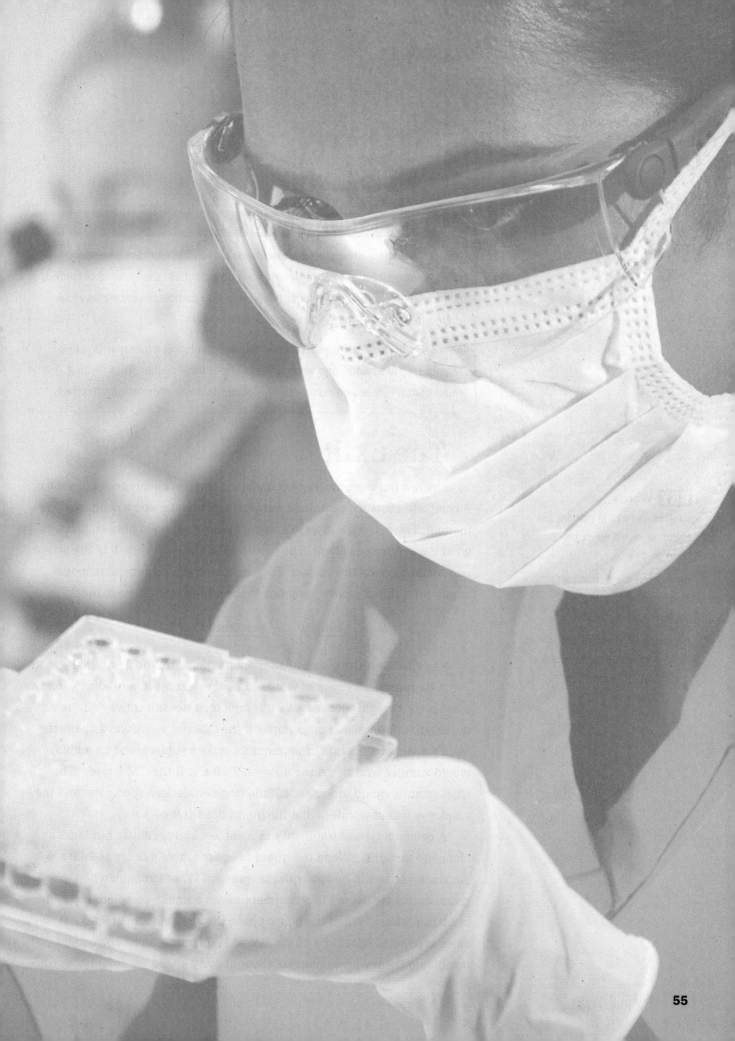

Writing Complete
Sentences

KEY *Words*

subject   what the sentence is about; always a noun, pronoun, or noun phrase

predicate   the action performed by or on the noun in the sentence; always a verb

fragment   a group of words that lacks a subject or a predicate or a complete thought

WorkKeys® in REAL LIFE

Insurance claims clerks review insurance claims and contact insured parties for additional information, among other duties. Documents prepared by insurance claims clerks must have clear and complete sentences to be understandable for their customers and coworkers.

Laboratory technicians assist scientists in monitoring experiments, keep logs to record results, and write reports about the findings. Their writing must contain clear and complete sentences to relay information effectively.

The Skill

To convey a business message completely, complete sentences are a must. A complete sentence contains a **subject**, a **predicate**, and a complete thought. The subject is always a noun, pronoun, or noun phrase. It states what the sentence is about. The predicate is always a verb. It is the action performed by or on the subject. For example, a store's general manager might write this complete sentence in the store's operations manual:

<u>subject</u>   <u>predicate</u>

The chief security <u>guard</u> always <u>opens</u> the store's doors at 9:00 A.M.

A **fragment** is a group of words that lacks a subject, a predicate, or a complete thought. Because it's incomplete, it doesn't convey all the necessary information. For example, if the GM wrote, "Always opens the store's doors at 9:00 A.M.," the fragment lacks a subject, and an employee would wonder *who* opens the doors at 9:00 A.M. If the GM wrote, "The chief security guard at 9:00 A.M.," the fragment lacks a predicate, and the employee would wonder what the guard *does* at 9:00 A.M.

A common type of fragment has a subject and predicate but lacks a complete thought: "When the guard opens the store's doors at 9:00 A.M." An employee would be left with the question *What happens when the guard opens the doors?* This fragment needs another, complete thought to make it clear: "When the guard opens the store's doors at 9:00 A.M., all sales associates should be on the floor." Fragments can be corrected by combining them with a complete thought or by adding or deleting words.

HERE'S HOW

What's the Job? Insurance claims clerks are responsible for preparing claims forms, writing letters to local contractors or auto repair shops, or writing letters requesting additional information from the insured party. The following is a letter to a homeowner who has filed a claim for fire damage.

Dear Mr. Adams:

We have received your claim for fire damage at 712 Maple Avenue. ❶ When you filed your claim, you neglected to include supporting evidence for the fine art that you have valued at $20,000.

To process your claim, we will need either receipts for the art or a ❷ videotape of your home showing the art for which you have placed a claim. As soon as we receive this information, we will begin to process your claim. Call me at the number below if you have questions. ❸

❶ This complete sentence has the subject *We*, the predicate *have received*, and a complete thought.

❷ Initially the clerk wrote, "To process your claim. We will need...." She fixed the fragment by adding it to the complete thought that follows.

❸ This sentence is complete even though it does not appear to have a subject. The subject of this sentence is understood to be *you*.

Read the following paragraph. Then, choose the sentence that is a fragment.

Mr. Adams has filed a claim for fire damage. In addition to damage to the building structure, he has claimed the loss of $20,000 worth of fine art. I have written to him. Requesting more information on the damaged and destroyed art. If he verifies the loss, I will honor the claim.

A. Mr. Adams has filed a claim for fire damage.
B. I have written to him.
C. Requesting more information on the damaged and destroyed art.

What Do I Need to Know? Look carefully at each sentence. Ask yourself which sentence lacks a subject, predicate, or complete thought.

- Choice A has a subject (*Mr. Adams*), predicate (*has filed*), and a complete thought.
- Choice B has a subject (*I*), predicate (*have written*), and a complete thought.
- Choice C has an incomplete predicate (*requesting*) but no subject: Who is doing the requesting? The answer is *C—Requesting more information on the damaged and destroyed art.*

Try It

Use a sheet of paper for these writing activities.

Activity 1 Read each passage. Then, choose the revision that best corrects the sentence fragment.

1. ABC Paper and Printing has introduced a new line of fine stationery, made exclusively for those with discriminating taste. <u>Made of cotton and linen, with fine texture.</u> The paper comes in a variety of rich colors to reflect your personal taste. Call us for a sample of this exceptional stationery.

   A. It is made of cotton and linen. Has a fine texture.
   B. Made of cotton and linen, it has a fine texture.
   C. Fine texture, it is made of cotton and linen.

2. We are sorry to hear that you are having problems with our digital camera, model XE70. Before you return it, we recommend that you try the following solutions. <u>First, the main problem.</u> Make sure the batteries are new and securely in place. Replacing old or insecurely placed batteries usually solves the problem. If this does not solve the problem, refer to the owner's manual, page 17, "Troubleshooting," for other suggestions.

   A. First, the main problem could be nonworking batteries.
   B. You should make sure the batteries are new and securely in place.
   C. If you replace old or insecurely placed batteries, this usually solves the problem.

What's the Job? Laboratory technicians often write reports of ongoing scientific experiments and events or problems that arise during the experiment. The following incident report was written by a laboratory technician.

Activity 2 Revise the following passage, correcting sentence fragments by combining sentences or adding or deleting words.

> **OVERVIEW: INCIDENT IN LAB 4 ON MARCH 19**
>
> The study on growing *E. coli* in three different media has been jeopardized. An incident that occurred on March 19. The incident began when a flaw was discovered in the glove worn by a lab technician. When the flaw, a small hole previously unnoticed, was discovered. The technician immediately changed gloves. However, he had previously handled sample 3, and it may have been contaminated. Because of this possible contamination, the experiment will need to be repeated.

See page 117 for sample answers.

Your Turn

Use your own paper to write a response to the prompt on this page. When writing your response, remember to follow the writing process.

Prewrite: Generate and list your ideas about the topic. Figure out what your main idea is. Then organize your ideas.

Draft: Write your draft using your ideas and your plan for organization. Write your main idea in a topic sentence near the beginning of the draft. **Write in complete sentences.**

Revise: Read your draft, looking for ways to improve it. **Check for fragments and revise where necessary.**

Edit: Read your draft again, looking for errors in grammar, spelling, capitalization, and punctuation.

Testing Tip

When revising your writing, read it silently and pause at each period. Is the group of words you just read a complete thought? If not, you've detected a fragment. Choose an effective way to fix it.

Prompt:

Your company has a policy of hiring workers for fewer than 30 hours per week so that it is not required to offer benefits like health insurance and sick leave. By doing so, the company says that it is able to provide living wages to a greater number of people. Critics argue that the company should hire fewer workers so that they can receive full benefits. As an employee in this company's human resources department, you have been asked to write a letter stating your opinion on this issue and your reasons for your opinion.

KEY POINTS

When writing for business:

➜ Make sure all your sentences have a subject and predicate.

➜ Reread your writing, checking for sentence fragments.

➜ Consider the best way to revise sentence fragments, such as adding the fragment to a complete thought or adding or deleting words.

See page 117 for a sample response.

Using Compound Sentences

KEYS TO...

Using Compound Sentences

When reading the lesson, keep the following points in mind:

➔ A compound sentence is composed of two independent clauses.

➔ The clauses are linked with a comma and coordinating conjunction or with a semicolon.

➔ Avoid run-on sentences and comma splices by writing compound sentences correctly.

WorkKeys® in REAL LIFE

Sales managers direct the distribution of products, plan staff training, and monitor customer preferences to determine the focus of sales efforts. Other duties include writing letters to customers and writing training materials and reports. Sales managers use compound sentences to relate their ideas clearly.

Occupational health and safety technicians collect data on work environments and evaluate programs to protect workers from biological, chemical, or physical hazards. These technicians write reports that use clear and effective compound sentences.

The Skill

Business writing often requires conveying complex ideas. Simple sentences usually convey simple ideas and can become monotonous to read. Compound sentences can express more complex ideas and make a business document read more smoothly.

A **compound sentence** contains two independent clauses, or simple sentences, joined by a comma and a **coordinating conjunction**. For example, a customer service representative might write, "The order was incomplete, so the customer was dissatisfied." Each clause can stand alone: The order was incomplete. The customer was dissatisfied. The writer joined the two clauses with a comma and the word *so*, signaling the cause-effect relationship between the two. The coordinating conjunctions are *and, but, or, yet, for, nor,* and *so*.

You may also use a semicolon to link two clauses in a compound sentence. However, independent clauses should not be linked without good reason; there should be a relationship between them.

A common business writing mistake is to run two independent clauses together without either a comma and coordinating conjunction or a semicolon. The resulting **run-on sentence** can lead to confusion. Two independent clauses run together with only a comma form a **comma splice**. You can correct a run-on sentence in your own business writing by using a period to create two sentences or by adding a coordinating conjunction.

KEY Words

compound sentence two independent clauses in one sentence

coordinating conjunction a word used to link independent clauses. To remember these conjunctions, think of the word FANBOYS: *for, and, nor, but, or, yet, so.*

run-on sentence two independent clauses run together incorrectly; when linked only with a comma, the run-on is called a **comma splice**

HERE'S HOW

What's the Job? Sales managers are responsible for writing sales reports, along with other documents. Read the excerpt from a report written by the sales manager of a computer software design company.

One of our best-selling products is the game Warlords of the West. It was released two weeks ago, and it has already doubled the sales of our previous best-selling game. We have just launched an aggressive ad ❶ campaign, so we expect continued high sales for the rest of this ❷ quarter. We have already begun designing *Warlords of the West and Beyond*. It will not be released until next year, but we may count on ❸ substantial presales.

❶ The independent clauses in this compound sentence are linked by a comma and the coordinating conjunction *and*.

❷ The coordinating conjunction *so* in this compound sentence indicates the cause-effect relationship between the independent clauses.

❸ The coordinating conjunction *but* in this compound sentence indicates the contrast relationship between the independent clauses.

The sales manager linked sentences with related ideas to form compound sentences. This sentence structure helps clarify ideas and makes the report more readable.

Read the following memo from a letter to a sales representative from her sales manager. Then, choose the run-on sentence.

We will be adding to our sales force next year. We want to expand your territory, but not until next spring. You will receive a substantial raise in pay, and you will also be given a promotion to Regional Sales Rep. We are excited to make you this offer. We hope you will accept this new assignment it is a great opportunity for you.

A. We will be adding to our sales force next year.

B. We want to expand your territory, but not until next spring.

C. We hope you will accept this new assignment it is a great opportunity for you.

What Do I Need to Know? Look carefully at each sentence. Which one has two independent clauses that are not joined with a comma and coordinating conjunction or with a semicolon?

- Choice A is a simple sentence.
- Choice B has only one independent clause, with a phrase attached.
- Choice C has two independent clauses with no comma or coordinating conjunction. The answer is *C—We hope you will accept this new assignment it is a great opportunity for you.*

Try It

Use a sheet of paper for these writing activities.

KEYS to Success

After writing a document on the job, read it and ask yourself: *Can simple sentences be combined effectively to make a compound sentence? Does this contain any run-on sentences?*

Activity 1 Rewrite each paragraph. Combine simple sentences into compound sentences if that will make the writing more effective. Fix comma splices and other run-ons.

1. This year's annual sales meeting will be held at Royal Hotel in New Orleans. As the meeting's social coordinator, I have planned a series of activities they should please all tastes. Details will be announced first we must finalize them. Anyone who has suggestions may call or e-mail me.

2. Our company is considering changing insurance providers. We would like you to submit a bid. We have thirty-five employees. Only one has a family. He has three young children. We want medical coverage for employees and owners. We also want to include dental insurance. Please send your bid before October 1. Call me if you have questions.

3. As many of you know, we will be installing a new computer system on November 1, training will begin as soon as installation is complete. The new system will make communications within the company easier. The system is faster. There will be less down time. We think you will be pleased with the change.

What's the Job? Occupational health and safety technicians report on safety conditions at plants and offices. The following excerpt is from a report by an occupational health and safety technician.

Activity 2 Revise the excerpt, combining simple sentences into compound sentences where appropriate and correcting run-on sentences and comma splices.

> **REPORT: CONDITIONS AT NATIONAL GAS PLANT 31**
> The conditions at Plant 31 are generally up to code. I did observe minor problems. There was only one important one. In building 5, area 12, pump valve handles appear to be wearing out and should be replaced. Repeat inspection will be necessary, this is a minor problem, but it could develop into a serious hazard. We should schedule another inspection, it should be done within three months.

See pages 117–118 for sample answers.

Your Turn

Use your own paper to write a response to the prompt on this page. When writing your response, remember to follow the writing process.

Prewrite: Generate and list your ideas about the topic. Then, organize your ideas.

Draft: Write your draft using your ideas and your plan for organization. **Use compound sentences, where appropriate, by combining sentences that have related ideas.**

Revise: Read your draft, looking for ways to improve it. **See if you can combine related ideas into compound sentences. Make sure that you have no run-on sentences and have used coordinating conjunctions properly.**

Edit: Read your draft again, looking for errors in grammar, spelling, capitalization, and punctuation.

> **Testing Tip**
>
> To combine two sentences into a compound sentence on a test response paper, write the comma between the two sentences, insert an appropriate coordinating conjunction with a caret (^), and lowercase the beginning letter of the second sentence.

Prompt:

You work for a company that values teamwork, and it rewards groups of employees who work together to reach a goal. The company recently announced that it plans to join a citywide softball league and is looking for players to join the team. The company has said that employees who participate will get an extra day off at the end of the summer. Some employees believe that employees should not be rewarded for outside-of-work activities. Management feels that this is just one of the many ways employees can be rewarded for teamwork and company spirit.

Write a memo to the company president explaining your views on the softball team plans. Be sure to give specific reasons for your opinions.

KEY POINTS

When writing for business:

→ Create compound sentences from simple sentences with related ideas.

→ Use a comma and a coordinating conjunction, or a semicolon, to make a compound sentence.

→ Make sure you have no run-on sentences: two simple sentences written together with no coordinating conjunction or with a comma only.

See page 118 for a sample response.

Using Complex Sentences

KEYS TO...

Using Complex Sentences

When reading the lesson, keep the following points in mind:

→ Complex sentences have one independent clause and one or more dependent, or subordinate, clauses.

→ Subordinate clauses add information to the main clause; they always begin with a subordinating conjunction or the words *that, who, which,* or *what.*

KEY *Words*

complex sentence an independent clause with one or more subordinate clauses

subordinate clause a clause that begins with a subordinating conjunction or relative pronoun and that has a subject and a predicate, but no complete thought

subordinating conjunction a word used at the beginning of a subordinate clause

---

WorkKeys® in REAL LIFE

Transportation managers plan and direct transportation operations within an organization. They also work with other managers to develop and put into effect policies related to transportation. They write memos, letters, and reports conveying instructions and ideas. Using complex sentences helps make their ideas understandable and their writing smooth.

Agricultural sciences professors teach dairy sciences, soil conservation, and other courses related to agriculture. In addition to teaching, they conduct research and publish their findings in professional journals. Using complex sentences helps them convey complex ideas in their writing.

The Skill

A string of simple sentences sounds choppy, while a number of long compound sentences can be repetitive. Good business writing includes a third type of sentence that helps make writing flow more smoothly and allows the writer to convey complex ideas.

A **complex sentence** has an independent clause, plus one or more dependent or **subordinate clauses**. A subordinate clause has a subject and predicate, but it is dependent upon an independent clause to make a complete thought. For example, a transportation manager may write in a report: "When the ice storm struck, many trucks were stranded after they slid off the highway." In the sentence, the independent clause is *many trucks were stranded.* It contains a complete thought. Both *When the ice storm struck* and *after they slid off the highway* are subordinate clauses. Neither can stand alone, but they each add a layer of complexity by adding more information.

A subordinate clause begins with a **subordinating conjunction**, such as *because, since, after, although,* or *when.* The conjunction shows the relationship between the two thoughts. Subordinate clauses may also begin with the relative pronouns *that, who, which,* or *what.*

A common business writing error is treating a subordinate clause as a complete sentence. The result is a sentence fragment. For example, *When the ice storm struck* is a fragment. You can correct a subordinate clause fragment by adding it to a main clause or deleting the subordinating conjunction.

What's the Job? Along with performing other duties, transportation managers write reports and memos. The following passage is from a memo written by a transportation manager.

> After the recent incident at the loading dock, we have decided to ❶ increase security. We will be adding additional lighting in the loading dock area, including motion-activated lights directly over the doors of each dock. When the new lighting system is in place, we will install a ❷ new alarm system. Incidents like the recent attempted break-in should be eliminated after these measures are taken. ❸

❶ Even though this phrase begins with the word *after*, it is not a subordinate clause because it does not have a subject and predicate.

❷ When a complex sentence begins with a subordinating conjunction, the subordinate clause must be separated from the main clause with a comma.

❸ When the subordinate clause comes after the main clause, a comma is usually not necessary to separate the two.

Read the following details of a memo from a transportation manager to the company president. Then, answer the question that follows.

> As of today, the blizzard in Colorado has shut down traffic on Highway 70. Because two of our trailers are stranded in Denver, the shipment of computers to Chicago retailers will be delayed. When the highway re-opens, we will inform the retailers of the expected delivery date. We will move this shipment as quickly as possible, and we will keep you informed of its status.

Which of these sentences is a complex sentence?

A. As of today, the blizzard in Colorado has shut down traffic on Highway 70.

B. Because two of our trailers are stranded in Denver, the shipment of computers to Chicago retailers will be delayed.

C. We will move this shipment as quickly as possible, and we will keep you informed of its status.

What Do I Need to Know? Ask yourself which sentence has a subordinate clause.

- Sentence A has an introductory phrase, but only one clause with a subject and predicate (*blizzard . . . has shut*).

- Sentence C has two independent clauses, each a complete thought (*We will move; we will keep*), but no subordinating clause.

- Sentence B has a subordinate clause beginning with *because*. It is a complex sentence. The answer is *B*.

Try It

Use a sheet of paper for these writing activities.

Activity 1 Read the following memo from the director of human resources. Then, write the answer to each item.

To All Employees:

Many of you have come to me with rumors about a reorganization of staff. Although it is true that we have planned reorganization, rumors about job loss are unfounded. Such rumors can be damaging to staff morale, so I will attempt to address as many of these issues as I can.

First of all, no one is in danger of losing his or her job. Some staff members will be moved from their current departments. Those with a technical background are most likely to be moved to a new team that deals only with technical issues. When the organization plan is finally in place. Most employees will remain in their current positions. No one will be out of a job, and salaries will remain the same.

Please see me personally to discuss any further questions.

1. Identify two complex sentences in this memo.
2. Identify a sentence fragment in this memo.
3. Write a revision of the fragment.

What's the Job? Agricultural sciences professors sometimes write articles in popular journals, written for the public, as well as in professional journals. The following is an excerpt from an article that an agricultural sciences professor wrote.

Activity 2 Read the passage. Then, write the complex sentence, underlining the subordinating conjunction. Write a revision for any sentence fragments.

ADAPTING CORN TO CLIMATE CHANGE

The Agricultural Research Service is currently working on a project to increase the adaptability and quality of corn, a staple in the world's food supply. The research focuses on developing adaptability to climate and resistance to insects and disease in corn. Because corn has been highly bred over the centuries, it currently has a small base of genes. This program will attempt to broaden the gene base by using tropical or other unusual maize genes. Because the world climate is changing. A new breed of corn that can adapt to a changing world is important.

See page 118 for sample answers.

Your Turn

Use your own paper to write a response to the prompt on this page. When writing your response, remember to follow the writing process.

Prewrite: Generate and list your ideas about the topic. Then, organize your ideas.

Draft: Write your draft using your ideas and your plan for organization. **Use complex sentences to develop your ideas and improve the readability of your writing.**

Revise: Read your draft, looking for ways to improve it. **Make sure all subordinate clauses are attached to a main clause.**

Edit: Read your draft again, looking for errors in grammar, spelling, capitalization, and punctuation.

Prompt:

The maintenance supervisor has written a memo complaining about the condition of the refrigerator in the kitchen. She states that frequently there is spoiled food left for too long and that employees who use the refrigerator do not keep it clean. Your coworkers also have been complaining that people often take food that is not theirs and do not clean up spills that occur when they put in or remove food. Write a memo to your coworkers that states your opinion on how the refrigerator should be used responsibly. Be as specific as possible with your recommendations.

Testing Tip

Read the prompt carefully and decide what sorts of supporting details you will need. Their relationship to the main idea is often a clue to what kind of subordinate ideas and conjunctions you will want to use. For example, if you are discussing the times to take action when using the refrigerator, you may want to use clauses beginning with *before, after,* and *when*.

KEY POINTS

When writing for business:

➜ Remember that complex sentences have one independent clause and one or more subordinate clauses.

➜ Always attach a subordinate clause to an independent clause.

➜ Use subordinate clauses to improve readability and to add complexity to ideas and information in the main clause.

See page 118 for a sample response.

Achieving
Sentence Variety

KEYS TO...

Achieving Sentence Variety

When reading the lesson, keep the following points in mind:

→ Using a variety of sentences makes your writing more interesting and readable.

→ Variety can be achieved by mixing long and short sentences, using different sentence structures, and using different sentence openings.

WorkKeys® in REAL LIFE

Financial managers, such as bank branch managers, have many duties, including overseeing the activities of bank employees, attracting new customers, and approving or rejecting applications for business or personal loans. Financial managers must be able to write clear, readable letters, memos, and reports. Using a variety of sentences helps achieve this.

Wildlife biologists study animals in their natural habitats and assess the effect of environments on animals. Some write journal articles, give presentations in schools, and create educational materials. Using a variety of sentences makes their writing understandable and appealing to their audience.

The Skill

Business writing does not have to be dull and boring. In fact, it shouldn't be. You can pass on information and get your point across more effectively—thereby scoring points with your supervisors—with lively writing.

Sentences of similar length and structure following one after the other can be deadening. For example, consider how you feel reading these sentences from a loan officer: "We received your application. It was reviewed promptly. We are pleased to tell you. We can approve your loan." A variety of sentence lengths and structures enlivens the writing: "We received your application, and it was reviewed promptly. We are pleased to tell you that we can approve your loan." The first two simple sentences were combined into a compound sentence. The last two were combined into a complex sentence.

A variety of sentence structures (simple, compound, complex) improves the flow of ideas. It also leads to different sentence lengths, which creates a rhythm to your writing. Simple sentences can be combined into compound sentences, complex sentences, and even compound-complex sentences.

A variety of sentence openings can also make your writing more readable. Some examples include opening with an adverb ("*Unfortunately,* we cannot approve your loan"); a prepositional phrase ("*For the first time,* our department has a 100% customer satisfaction ranking"); a **gerund** ("*Being* late for work may be cause for dismissal"); and a **participial phrase** ("*Impressed by your proposal,* my company grants you the project").

KEY Words

gerund an *-ing* form of a verb used as a noun, as in the subject of a sentence

participial phrase a group of words beginning with the *-ing* or *-ed* form of a verb, used as an adjective

HERE'S HOW

What's the Job? Financial managers write letters, memos, and reports. Read this excerpt from a promotional letter written by a bank manager to a local small business.

Being a small business owner, you may often have cash flow problems, especially at the end of the month. When the end of the month arrives, ❶ you have bills to pay, and you have payroll to meet. Our new program, ❷ Bonus Cash, can help solve those cash problems. With this program, you may write checks for up to $10,000 over your balance in your business checking account. Let us help with Bonus Cash. Call me for more information. ❸

❶ This sentence begins with a participial phrase that modifies the subject *you*.

❷ This is a compound-complex sentence.

❸ These two simple sentences balance the previous long sentences and add emphasis to the ideas in these sentences.

Read the following memo. Then, choose the revision that best keeps the main idea while using a variety of sentences.

The Bonus Cash program is popular. We have gained five new business customers this month. We met with them personally. This program will attract more new customers with continued promotion.

A. The *Bonus Cash* program is popular. We have gained five new business customers this month, meeting with them personally. With continued promotion, this program will attract more new customers.

B. The *Bonus Cash* program is popular, and we have gained five new business customers this month. Meeting with them personally, this program will attract more new customers if we continue promotion.

C. The *Bonus Cash* program is popular. As we gained five new business customers this month, we met with them personally, so this program will attract more new customers with continued promotion.

What Do I Need to Know? Look carefully at each revision. Ask how effectively each has combined thoughts. Ask how each sounds as you read it.

- Option A combines sentences effectively and revises the opening of the last sentence.
- Option B creates a complex sentence, but the introductory *Meeting with them personally* does not modify the subject *program*.
- Option C combines the sentences into a long-winded compound-complex sentence that uses *we* as a subject twice.
- The answer is *A*. It is the best revision.

Common Error Alert

When using participial phrases, make sure that the subject of your sentence directly follows the phrase. Otherwise, you will have a dangling modifier. For example, in *Being a small business owner, cash flow problems often arise*, the subject is *cash flow problems*. *Being a small business owner* doesn't modify *problems*; it is a participial phrase left dangling, with nothing to modify.

Try It

Use a sheet of paper for these writing activities.

Activity 1 Read the following memo from a store manager to store employees. Then, respond to each item that follows.

(1) As you know, next Friday is Black Friday, the day after the Thanksgiving holiday. (2) This year we expect record sales. (3) We have deep discounts on electronic items. (4) We also have specials on this year's popular toys. (5) Holiday items are also discounted. (6) Holiday clothing is discounted too.

(7) We will open our doors at 4:00 A.M. (8) We expect all employees to report by 3:30 A.M. (9) This will be a difficult day. (10) In the past, as you know, there have been some incidents with disgruntled customers. (11) Frustrated by the crowd, tempers will be short. (12) We will not tolerate any rudeness to our customers. (13) We will have extra security guards on duty. (14) Report any problems to them immediately. (15) We hope this will be our best year yet.

1. Revise sentences 4 to 6 to make this section read smoothly.
2. Revise sentences 7 and 8 to achieve sentence variety.
3. Revise the sentence with the dangling modifier.
4. Revise sentences 12 to 14 to achieve sentence variety.

What's the Job? Wildlife biologists may write educational materials for the public. This excerpt is from a pamphlet written by a wildlife biologist.

Activity 2 Read the passage. Then, write a revision, using a variety of sentences and sentence openings.

THE WOLF IN THE WILD

The center of the wolf's life is the pack. The "lone wolf" is not a happy wolf. The pack is its family. The pack is its society. The pack has a leader and followers. Each wolf knows its place in the pack.

Wolves range across a wide area while hunting. They often get separated. Humans keep in touch across miles by phone, letters, and the Internet. Wolves have a unique way of communicating with the family. They howl. Every human has a unique voice. Every wolf has a unique howl. It is recognized by pack members. The wolf howl carries over great distances. The sound can travel across a tundra and through a forest. The howl calls the pack together.

See pages 118–119 for sample answers.

Your Turn

Use your own paper to write a response to the prompt on this page. When writing your response, remember to follow the writing process.

Prewrite: Generate and list your ideas about the topic. Then, organize your ideas.

Draft: Write your draft using your ideas and your plan for organization. **Use a variety of sentence structures, lengths, and openings.**

Revise: Read your draft, looking for ways to improve it. **Combine simple sentences to make compound or complex sentences, or combine the ideas in compound or complex sentences to make a simple sentence where appropriate.**

Edit: Read your draft again, looking for errors in grammar, spelling, capitalization, and punctuation. **Be sure you have no dangling modifiers.**

Testing Tip

After writing your draft, read it so that you hear the sentences in your head. Listen for choppiness, repetition, and monotony. Those are the sentences you will want to revise.

Prompt:

Your employer has always made annual flu shots available in the nurse's office for those workers who want them. This year, the company is considering making the vaccine mandatory for all workers unless there is a medical condition that makes it unadvisable. Your employer wants to have a safe, healthy, productive workplace and believes that mandating the flu vaccine is a good step toward that goal. Others feel that health care is a private matter that cannot be mandated in a workplace. Write a letter to your employer stating whether or not you think making the flu vaccine mandatory is a good idea. Support your point of view.

KEY POINTS

When writing for business:

→ Use a variety of sentence structures to make your writing interesting and readable.

→ Vary your sentence openings by using different types of phrases.

→ Combine simple sentences when appropriate.

GOING FOR THE GOLD   For the Unit 4 Assessment and the Online Posttest, go to www.mysteckvaughn.com/CAREER.

See page 119 for a sample response.

Achieving Sentence Variety   **71**

Unit 5
Grammar, Usage, and Mechanics

Preschool teachers nurture young children, helping them grow and develop. Creating educational games and storytelling are just two of the ways in which they stimulate preschoolers' minds and spark their imagination. As part of their responsibilities, preschool teachers also must write. They share information in writing with supervisors, other teachers, and parents. To convey a competent, professional image, this information must be free of errors in grammar, usage, and mechanics.

In your job, you also want your writing to convey a professional image. Careful editing of your memos, e-mails, and reports will help you detect errors in grammar, misspellings, and punctuation and capitalization mistakes that detract from your writing and distract your coworkers or boss from the content of your message. Even worse, these mistakes convey the impression that you are not careful about details. The lessons in this unit will provide practice in these writing skills:

→ **Lesson 15**   Making Subjects and Verbs Agree

→ **Lesson 16**   Using the Correct Verb

→ **Lesson 17**   Keeping Tenses Consistent

→ **Lesson 18**   Using Pronouns Correctly

→ **Lesson 19**   Using Punctuation

→ **Lesson 20**   Spelling Correctly

→ **Lesson 21**   Using Capitalization

Would you wear dirty, scruffy clothing on a job interview? Of course you wouldn't. Likewise, you want your writing to look its best. Attending to grammar, usage, and mechanics will help ensure that your writing, like you, looks its best on the job.

Making Subjects and
Verbs Agree

KEYS TO...

Making Subjects and Verbs Agree

When reading the lesson, keep the following points in mind:

→ Subjects and verbs must agree in number.

→ When editing to make subjects and verbs agree, change the verb so that it is the same number—singular or plural—as the subject.

WorkKeys® in REAL LIFE

School principals plan and direct the activities and staffs of elementary or secondary level schools. To do their jobs, they must write letters, memos, reports, evaluations, and other documents. Correct grammar, including subject and verb agreement, is essential in their writing.

Materials engineers evaluate materials, develop new uses for materials, and monitor material performance. Materials engineers write memos, letters, and reports regarding their work. Making subjects and verbs agree is important in making their writing clear.

The Skill

One of the most common errors in business writing occurs with subject-verb agreement. Subjects and verbs must agree in number. That is, a singular subject must have a singular verb (The <u>invoice</u> <u>is</u> due); a plural subject must have a plural verb (The <u>invoices</u> <u>are</u> due). Here are a few of the most important guidelines in making subjects and verbs agree:

- If the subject consists of two or more nouns or pronouns (a **compound subject**) connected by *and*, use a plural verb: *Angela and Ross are the new employees.*
- If the compound subject is connected by *or* or *nor*, use a singular verb: *Neither Angela nor Ross is trained.*
- If a subject is a **collective noun**—a noun that names a group of people or things—make the verb singular if the group is acting as a unit: *The committee is meeting tomorrow morning. The staff works late on Mondays.*
- When a phrase comes between the subject and the verb, make the verb agree with the subject, not the noun in the phrase: *One of the trainees is leaving. The supervisors, with the exception of Harry Blunt, are getting transferred.*
- The following words always require a singular verb when used as a subject: *each, either, neither, everyone, everybody, anyone, anybody, nobody, somebody, someone.*

KEY Words

compound subject a subject composed of two or more nouns or pronouns, connected by the words *and, or,* or *nor*

collective noun a noun that names a group of people or things, but is treated as singular, such as *committee, band, staff, team, family*

HERE'S HOW

What's the Job? School principals sometimes write newsletters to keep students, parents, and teaching staff informed about their school. Read the following excerpt from a letter written by a principal.

As the school year begins, the faculty and I want to welcome all the ❶ students, especially those new to Parnell High School. Our entire student body welcomes you newcomers, and we will do everything we ❷ can to make you feel at home. Each of you is important to us. ❸

We have exciting plans for extracurricular activities this year. Our school band is already practicing for this year's football season. ❷ Everyone in the band is looking forward to having some new members. ❸ Members of the band are going to be here after school hours on ❹ Friday to welcome anyone who wants to learn more about the band program.

❶ The compound subject takes a plural verb.

❷ *Student body* and *school band* are collective nouns and have singular verbs.

❸ *Each* and *everyone* are singular and take singular verbs.

❹ In this case, *members* is the subject, not *band*, so the verb is plural.

Read the following excerpt of a letter from a school principal to parents. Then, choose the clause that has an error in subject-verb agreement.

Some parents have complained about the new dress code instituted this year. The dress code is flexible, but certain types of clothing is not allowed. Dress codes are always going to be questioned by some students and parents, but the dress code committee, along with other staff members, believes this code is fair to all students.

A. The dress code is flexible
B. certain types of clothing is not allowed
C. but the dress code committee, along with other staff members, believes this code is fair

What Do I Need to Know? Isolate the subject and verb of each sentence.
- A has a singular subject (*code*) and singular verb (*is*).
- C has a collective-noun subject (*committee*) and a singular verb (*believes*). Although the noun preceding the verb is plural (*members*), it is part of a phrase separating the subject from the verb.
- B has a plural subject (*types*, not *clothing*, which is part of a phrase separating the subject from the verb), but a singular verb (*believes*). The answer is *B—certain types of clothing is not allowed.*

Try It

Use a sheet of paper for these writing activities.

Activity 1 Write *OK* if the paragraph is without errors in subject-verb agreement. If there is an error in a sentence, write the sentence on your paper and underline the subject and the verb. Then, edit the sentence.

1. The first meeting of the PTA will be in the gymnasium on September 15. Committees are forming now for the coming year. The dress code committee is in need of members, as is the curriculum advisory committee.

2. Football season this year promises to be exciting. Our schedule is challenging, but the team is exceptionally well staffed. Mr. Taylor and Mr. Higgins, offensive coach and defensive coach respectively, has worked out a practice schedule. See Mr. Taylor for the team lineup and schedule.

3. As you know, there is a ballot proposal for a slight tax increase to benefit our schools. The tax will cover several important expenditures necessary to keep the schools up-to-date. Funds from this increase is intended for a new roof on the high school and for programs to update some of the classrooms. A student representative and a school staff representative is scheduled to be at each voting site to hand out flyers supporting this initiative.

What's the Job? Materials engineers are responsible for writing reports, among other duties. The following is an excerpt from a recommendation report written by a materials engineer to the board of directors of his company.

Activity 2 Read the excerpt. Then, edit the paragraph, correcting any errors in subject-verb agreement.

As board members are aware, biomaterials and nanotechnology is the cutting edge of materials technology in the medical field. Orthopedic implants and vascular implants are currently made of synthetic materials. These materials has a limited lifetime, and some implants begin to fail after only five years. Materials technology currently in use do not promote proper cellular regeneration around the implant, leading to a breakdown in the effectiveness of the implant. Nanotechnology is an exciting and promising field for the development of medical products. An increase in R&D funds are recommended to begin development of these products.

See page 119 for sample answers.

⋯⋯Your Turn⋯⋯

Use your own paper to write a response to the prompt on this page. When writing your response, remember to follow the writing process.

Prewrite: Generate and list your ideas about the topic. Then organize your ideas.

Draft: Write your draft using your ideas and your plan for organization. **As you write, be aware of subject-verb agreement in your sentences.**

Revise: Read your draft, looking for ways to improve it.

Edit: Read your draft again, looking for errors in grammar, spelling, capitalization, and punctuation. **Correct errors in subject-verb agreement by changing the verb to singular or plural as required.**

Testing Tip

Leave enough time after drafting and revising to edit your writing. Part of editing is making sure to identify the subject of each sentence and checking to see that the verb agrees in number.

Prompt:

For as long as you have been working at a company, its policy was that vacation time could not be carried over from year to year. In other words, if you had not taken all of your vacation time by December 31, you would lose whatever days you had left. After some complaints from employees, your human resources (HR) department is reconsidering this policy. It may allow employees to bank vacation time.

Write a letter to the HR department explaining your opinion on this proposed change in vacation policy

KEY POINTS

When writing for business:

➔ Make sure subjects and verbs agree in number.

➔ Correct errors in subject-verb agreement by making the verb singular or plural as needed.

See page 119 for a sample response.

Using the Correct Verb

KEYS TO...

Using the Correct Verb

When reading the lesson, keep these points in mind:

→ Verb tenses indicate when actions take place.

→ The perfect verb tenses use auxiliary, or helping, verbs.

→ The correct form of regular and irregular verbs must be used with auxiliary verbs.

WorkKeys® in REAL LIFE

Mental health counselors help individuals achieve optimum mental health. They guide clients to develop strategies for dealing with stress or problems with self-esteem, and they collect information about clients through interviews and observations. They must be able to write clear letters and reports with correct verb usage.

Industrial engineers coordinate and implement quality control and confer with clients, staff, and management regarding purchases, products, and product specifications. To communicate information and decisions, they must write clearly and effectively, using verbs correctly.

The Skill

Just as employees do much of the work in a company, the verb does much of the work in a sentence. Not only does it tell the action, but it also tells the time, or **tense**, of that action. The incorrect usage of verbs can cause confusion or misunderstanding, leaving a negative impression with your coworkers, your employer, or your company's clients. Following some basic rules about verb usage can help keep your writing free from errors.

The following chart shows some verb tenses and the **verb forms** used to build those tenses.

Present	Past	Future	Past Participle	Present Participle
talk	talked	will talk	talked	talking
go	went	will go	gone	going

Walked is a **regular verb**; its past and past participle are formed by adding *-ed*. *Write* is an **irregular verb**; it does not follow this usual pattern.

Perfect tenses are formed using the participle and an auxiliary (or helping) verb, usually *has* or *have* in the present perfect ("I have left the papers on your desk") and *had* in the past perfect ("I had gone before he came"). A common error is omitting the auxiliary verb in the past or present perfect tense, writing "I done the work" rather than "I have done the work."

Another common error is using the auxiliary with the wrong verb form, writing "I have went to the office" rather than "I have gone to the office."

KEY Words

tense the time that a verb expresses, such as present, past, or future

verb forms the forms (or spellings) that a verb takes. The principal verb forms are the *present* (or *base form*), the *past*, and the *past participle*.

regular verb a verb that forms its past and participle by adding *-ed* or *-ing: work/worked/working*

irregular verb a verb that does not follow the regular pattern of adding *-ed* or *-ing: do/did/done/doing*

HERE'S HOW

What's the Job? Mental health counselors guide individuals who have problems. They write evaluations and letters to clients or their clients' guardians. The following excerpt from a letter might have been written by a mental health counselor to the teacher of a young client.

> I hope that we will meet about Jon Harris tomorrow. By then I ❶ will have completed his evaluation. This morning I went over the ❷ ❸ file you sent me, covering the first half of the year. From his records, I see that Jon had achieved an impressive increase in his grade point ❹ average by the end of the first quarter, but now his work has begun to slip.

❶ The simple future tense tells when the action will take place.

❷ The future perfect tense tells that the action will have been done by a specified time in the future.

❸ The simple past tense shows an action happened in the past. *Go* is an irregular verb (*go/went/gone*).

❹ The past perfect tense tells that an action was finished by a specified time in the past.

Read the following letter from a mental health counselor to the parents of a client. Then, respond to the questions that follow.

> I have met with Sonia Appleton, Jon's guidance counselor at Camden High School. We discussed the difficulties Jon has with his peers and his recent decline in grades. We both agree that Jon is capable of being an A student. I would like to meet with you about Jon. I have reviewed his school files, including grades and incident reports, and yesterday I did thorough interviews with his teachers. They have gave me a good idea of the issues he has been facing.

Which of the following has an error in verb usage?

A. I have met with Sonia Appleton.
B. Yesterday I did thorough interviews.
C. They have gave me a good idea.

What Do I Need to Know? Check the tenses, making sure that the tense agrees with the time frame mentioned and that the correct verb form is used.

- In A, the tense is the present perfect. The correct auxiliary (*have*) is used, and the correct past participle form of *meet* (*met*) is used.
- In B, the word yesterday is a clue that the tense is the simple past. The word *did* is the past tense of the irregular verb *do*.
- In C, the tense is the present perfect The correct auxiliary (*have*) is used, but not the correct past participle form of *give*. The sentence should be "They have given me a good idea." The answer is *C*.

Try It

Use a sheet of paper for these writing activities.

Activity 1 Write *OK* if the underlined sentence has the correct verb. If there is an error in the sentence, rewrite the sentence, correcting the error.

1. As most of you know, our student drop-out rate has declined. <u>It had been as high as 25% in past years.</u> Today, we are proud to announce that the drop-out rate has shrunk to less than 10%. Of course, we will not be happy until every student who enrolls in this school graduates.

2. The training session for new employees will be held beginning next week. We have designed the session around the new department staffing. <u>I had hoped we could use the current training materials, but since we now have a new department, we have did some extensive revision on the program.</u> We think the new materials will be very effective.

3. <u>The Newton Institute been training people for careers in the trades and technology since 1987.</u> Now, we are changing our name—we will be known as Newton Technical Institute. <u>Although our name has changed, our mission remained the same today as always</u>—to prepare people for the world of today by training them in the jobs of tomorrow.

What's the Job? Industrial engineers confer with clients regarding manufacturing methods. The following letter was written by an industrial engineer to a client.

Activity 2 Read the letter. Then, edit it to correct any verb errors.

> Dear Mr. Huffstedt:
>
> Our team recently visits your plant to assess your manufacturing process. We would like to recommend reorganizing your manufacturing process along the lines of what is known as "Lean Manufacturing." We would use quantitative analysis tools to make a transformation, which could have reduced the environmental impact of your process as well.
>
> As you may know, Lean Manufacturing is also known as the TPS method, after its development by Toyota engineers in Japan. When applying this process, we will systematically have eliminated waste in eight areas, from production and transportation to human resources.
>
> We would like to meet with you to discuss this further. After we had an initial chat, we will submit a detailed proposal for your reorganization.

KEYS to Success

If verb forms or tenses give you difficulty, take the time to learn and practice using verbs correctly. Identify those verbs that give you problems and learn their forms. Pages 104–105 have some information on verbs, their forms, and their tenses; other reference books will help you too.

See page 120 for sample answers.

···· Your Turn ····

Use your own paper to write a response to the prompt on this page. When writing your response, remember to follow the writing process.

Prewrite: Generate and list your ideas about the topic. Then, organize your ideas.

Draft: Write your draft using your ideas and your plan for organization. **Use verbs that clearly relate the sequence of actions and are the correct forms.**

Revise: Read your draft, looking for ways to improve it.

Edit: Read your draft again, looking for errors in grammar, spelling, capitalization, and punctuation. **Look closely for errors in verb tense and verb form.**

Testing Tip

Read through the writing prompt slowly and carefully. If it asks you to give an opinion on an issue, don't spend too much time thinking it over. Pick a side and support your position with details and concrete examples.

Prompt:

The factory you work at runs twenty-four hours a day, with three different shifts. It is possible for most of the workers to reach the factory via public transportation, which allows them a safe, reliable, and inexpensive commute. However, for the very late shift, public transportation is not running. Those workers have to either drive or take more expensive forms of transportation. Those late-shift employees have stated to management that they should be paid more in order to compensate them for this extra expense. They argue that they do the same work as the earlier shifts, yet it costs them more to do the job.

Write a letter to management explaining whether you think late-shift workers should be paid more to make up for transportation costs.

KEY POINTS

When writing for business:

➡ Make sure you use the verb tense that correctly indicates the time of the action.

➡ Make sure you use the correct auxiliary verb for the perfect verb tenses.

➡ Make sure you have used the correct regular or irregular verb form for the verb tense you are expressing.

See page 120 for a sample response.

Keeping Tenses
Consistent

KEYS TO...

Keeping Tenses Consistent

When reading the lesson, keep the following points in mind:

→ In general, maintain the same verb tense throughout a piece of writing.

→ Shift verb tenses when a change in the time that actions or events take place occurs.

→ Shift verb tenses when you are adding information from another time.

KEY *Words*

consistent the same throughout an entire piece. For more information about verb tenses, see the Business Writer's Reference page 105.

WorkKeys® in REAL LIFE

Office clerks perform a variety of duties to keep an office running smoothly. One duty is to write letters to customers and memos to other staff. Clerks need to convey information clearly about the timing of events, which requires using appropriate verb tenses.

Electronics technicians work with electrical engineers to help design, develop, and test equipment, such as medical monitoring devices. On the job they write evaluations of equipment and memos to the engineer. These documents must present information in a logical sequence, using consistent verb tenses.

The Skill

If a business communication switches back and forth between past, present, and future without good reason, readers get confused. Important information can be misunderstood. Keeping verb tenses **consistent** is essential to clear writing.

If you use the simple past tense in telling an account, in general keep the simple past tense throughout. For example, an office clerk began a letter to an office machine supplier: "When we *bought* the photocopier six months ago, it *runs* just fine. However, we *used* it for barely a month when things *started* to go wrong." The present tense used in the main clause of the first sentence (*runs*) is inconsistent with the past tense used in the introductory subordinate clause (bought). The phrase *six months ago* is a clue that the past tense is needed. When editing her letter, the clerk changed *runs* to *ran*. She also changed *used* to *had used*.

Shift tenses when the actions or events you begin to write about take place at a different time. Look how the office clerk shifted tenses in her letter: "First numerous paper jams *occurred*. Then "ghost" images *began* appearing. Now the toner *does* not *affix* to the paper." The word *now* is a clue that the tense should change to the present. Use time-related words and phrases as a guide to which tense to use and when to shift tenses.

Also shift tenses when you add information from another time: "We *were informed* by your sales representative that we *can get* this copier replaced under warranty at no cost."

HERE'S HOW

What's the Job? Office clerks are responsible for answering phones, ordering supplies, and writing memos to staff or letters to customers. The following letter was written by an office clerk.

Dear Mr. Hammond:

I am so sorry that your shipment arrived in damaged **❶ ❷** condition. When we ship orders, we routinely protect fragile **❶ ❶** items with appropriate protective wrapping. Unfortunately, your shipment was packed incorrectly. We will ship you a **❷ ❸** replacement order today.

---

❶ The writer uses the simple present tense to express a condition (*sorry*) or events (*ship, protect*) that habitually occur.

❷ These statements express events that happened in the past (*arrived, was packed*).

❸ This statement states an event (*will ship*) that will happen in the future.

The office clerk changed tenses intentionally to express a chain of events past, present, and future: *I am; shipment arrived; we ship; we routinely protect; shipment was packed; We will ship.*

Read the following details in a memo from an office clerk. Then, respond to the question that follows.

Mr. James asked me to remind all of you that we are currently in "austerity mode." That means we are conserving as much as possible in all areas. I am ordering office supplies today and needed your requests. When these supplies are gone, we will not order again until next month.

Which statement uses verb tenses inconsistently?

A. Mr. James asked me to remind all of you that we are currently in "austerity mode."

B. I am ordering office supplies today and needed your requests.

C. When these supplies are gone, we will not order again until next month.

What Do I Need to Know? Look at each sentences to see which tense makes sense and whether a shift is necessary.

- In sentence A, *currently* is a clue that the present tense *are* is correct.

- In sentence C, *when* describes a situation that will take place in the future, so the shift to *will . . . order* is correct.

- In sentence B, *today* tells you the present *am ordering* is correct; there is no need to shift to the past *needed*. The correct answer is *B*.

Try It

Use a sheet of paper for these writing activities.

Activity 1 Each paragraph contains one or more underlined sentences containing a shift in tense. If the shift correctly adds information or expresses the chain of events, write *OK*. If the shift is unnecessary or incorrectly expresses a chain of events, edit the sentence(s) to correct the error.

1. Our business depends upon customer satisfaction. We are proud that our employees give outstanding customer service. (1) <u>However, we are surprised to get a phone call yesterday complaining that one of our representatives was rude to the caller in a recent conversation.</u> This lapse in customer service disappoints us, but we are sure that it is the exception to the rule.

2. The recent hurricane caused enormous damage. Our warehouse was completely demolished. Most of the contents of the warehouse were not salvageable. Our attached offices also suffered considerable damage. (2) <u>We are assessing the damage, trying to determine the dollar cost of this loss.</u> (3) <u>We will have the damage report soon.</u>

3. Highway 70 between Blair Avenue and Turner Street will be closed for repairs on Saturday and Sunday. (4) <u>Traffic is diverted to Hanley Avenue.</u> This will irritate motorists, but the closure will not disrupt traffic during rush hour. The weather will be good, and we will be able to make the repairs in two days.

What's the Job? Electronics technicians may need to write reports for the engineers with whom they work. Following is an excerpt from such a report.

Activity 2 Read the report. Then, correct any verb tense errors.

PRELIMINARY HOME HEALTH DEVICE REPORT

I tested the new design for the Early Warning Cardio Home Health device. The original design had serious problems in detecting measurable electrical resistance through the electrodes. The problem in the new design is that of relaying a sufficient level of electrical impulse through the electrodes attached to the patient's chest. Boosting the electrical impulse is the simplest way to solve the problem. However, my tests show that a redesign of the electrodes was needed as soon as possible to handle this additional electrical charge. In addition, field tests will be needed at some point to ensure that patients were able to tolerate the higher levels.

See page 120 for sample answers.

Your Turn

Use your own paper to write a response to the prompt on this page. When writing your response, remember to follow the writing process.

Prewrite: Generate and list your ideas about the topic. Then organize your ideas.

Draft: Write your draft using your ideas and your plan for organization. **Think about the time sequence in your draft and use the appropriate verb tenses.**

Revise: Read your draft, looking for ways to improve it. **Add information using a different verb tense if appropriate.**

Edit: Read your draft again, looking for errors in grammar, spelling, capitalization, and punctuation. **Edit for consistent verb tenses.**

Testing Tip

Read through the writing prompt slowly and carefully. Letters stating an opinion are often written in the present tense, using past or future tense where appropriate to give reasons for a position (what happened in the past or what will happen in the future).

Prompt:

Your company is considering changing its recommended retirement age from 62 to 60. In the letter sent to all employees, the chief executive officer stated that the average age of the company's workforce has been rising steadily over the past decade. He believes that a business needs younger workers with fresh perspectives to keep the company viable. Others in the company argue that 62 is still young and that experience is as important as youth.

Write a letter to the CEO explaining your point of view on the retirement age.

KEY POINTS

When writing for business:

→ In general, keep verb tenses consistent.

→ Shift verb tense when the time frame of actions or events changes.

→ Shift verb tense to add information from a different time frame.

See pages 120–121 for a sample response.

Using Pronouns
Correctly

KEYS TO...

Using Pronouns Correctly

When reading the lesson, keep the following points in mind:

→ Pronouns may be used as subjects or objects in a sentence.

→ Pronouns must have a clear antecedent.

→ Pronouns must agree in number with their antecedents.

KEY *Words*

antecedent the noun for which a pronoun stands

subject pronoun a pronoun that takes the subject position in a sentence: *I, you, he, she, it, we, they, who*

object pronoun a pronoun that takes the object position in a sentence (direct object or object of a preposition): *me, you, him, her, it, us, them, whom*

For more information about pronouns, see the Business Writer's Reference page 105.

WorkKeys® in REAL LIFE

Environmental compliance inspectors investigate violations of environmental regulations and write reports based on their investigations. Using pronouns correctly helps them to present information clearly.

Legal secretaries prepare legal documents, schedule appointments, and also write letters to clients and memos to staff. It is essential that legal secretaries use pronouns correctly to avoid confusion in legal issues.

·····The Skill·····

A pronoun replaces a noun. The noun is called the pronoun's **antecedent**. Here are some basic rules to help you use pronouns correctly on the job:

- Use a **subject pronoun** as a subject or as a predicative nominative (a pronoun that comes after the verb but names the same person or thing as the subject): *Anna, the administrative assistant, answers the phone here.* **She** *answers the phone.* (subject) *The administrative assistant is* **she**. (predicate nominative)

- Use an **object pronoun** as a direct or indirect object or as the object of a preposition: *Anna takes phone messages. Anna gives* **them** *to Ms. Vigil.* (direct object) *Anna gives* **her** *the messages.* (indirect object). *Anna gives the messages to* **her**. (object of the preposition *to*)

- Match pronouns and antecedents in number. Use a singular pronoun for a singular antecedent and a plural pronoun for a plural antecedent: *Give each employee a time card that* **he** *or* **she** *will punch.* (not "that they will punch") *Give all the employees time cards that* **they** *will punch.*

Here are some common mistakes business writers make with pronouns:

- "Anna and Jen conferred, and then she left for the day." The antecedent is unclear. Who's *she*? Edit to read: ". . . then Anna left for the day" or ". . . then Jen left for the day."

- "Me and him went to the meeting." The two pronouns are subjects. Edit to read: "He and I went to the meeting."

- "Let's keep this information between you and I." The pronouns are both objects of the preposition *between*. Edit to read: "between you and me."

HERE'S HOW

What's the Job? Environmental compliance inspectors must write reports about their investigations into possible violations of laws and regulations. Read the following excerpt from a report written by an environmental compliance inspector.

> I interviewed Jana Andrews and Jeff Adams, owners of AA Auto, regarding the violations reported. The owners insist that they dispose of used motor oil in accordance with the ordinance. ❶ Despite these assertions from both her and him, violations have ❷ been reported by several customers, who say that they have ❸ witnessed the owners pouring oil into the common sewer drain.

❶ The pronoun *they* has a clear antecedent—*owners*. Both *they* and *owners* are plural. The subject pronoun *they* is the subject of the clause *they dispose.* . . .

❷ The object pronouns *her* and *him* are objects of the preposition *from.* The antecedent of *her* is *Jana Andrews*; the antecedent of *him* is *Jeff Adams*.

❸ The pronoun *who* has the antecedent *customers.* It is the subject of the clause *who say. Customers* is plural; *who* may be either singular or plural.

Read the following details of a report. Then choose the best revision of the underlined sentence.

> The Environmental Protection Agency has issued a report alerting compliance inspectors to violations at large universities. They are widespread, and they operate much like small cities, with research laboratories, power plants, and wastewater treatment plants, and it can cause serious damage.

A. Violations are widespread. They can cause serious damage because universities operate much like small cities, with research laboratories, power plants, and wastewater treatment plants.

B. They are widespread. Universities operate much like small cities, with their research laboratories, power plants, and wastewater treatment plants. They can cause serious damage.

C. Universities are widespread, and they operate much like small cities, with research laboratories, power plants, and wastewater treatment plants, and they can cause serious damage.

What Do I Need to Know? Look carefully at each revision to see if each pronoun has a clear antecedent and is used correctly

- Option B does not clarify the antecedent of *they*.
- Option C mistakenly replaces the first *they* with *universities* and does not clarify the antecedent of the last *they*.
- Option A clearly identifies the antecedent of *They* by placing the pronoun directly following its antecedent, *Violations*, and removes the unclear pronoun *it*. The answer is *A*.

Try It

Use a sheet of paper for these writing activities.

KEYS to Success

Use nouns when possible to keep your meaning clear. Replace nouns with pronouns when repeating the noun would sound awkward or repetitive. Using people's names rather then pronouns in business writing personalizes your writing.

Activity 1 Explain the pronoun error in each of the underlined sentences. Then rewrite the sentence, correcting the error. Sentences may have more than one error.

1. We have received reports of violations at the waste treatment plant in the town of Delta, Louisiana. <u>Me and Mike are going to drive down there to investigate it.</u>

2. Lead-based paint is one of the most common hazards in older buildings. <u>A child living in an older building often ingests it, causing serious developmental damage to them.</u>

3. Water discharged into the Rock River from the paper plant in town may contain unacceptable levels of various chemicals. <u>We are sending a team of investigators to see if it can be solved, but both the director and me think we will have to issue a citation.</u>

4. We will be attending a symposium sponsored by the EPA on the new Audit Policy. It allows institutions to make voluntary disclosures of noncompliance, thus avoiding more severe penalties. <u>The primary presenter at the symposium is the assistant director of the EPA, and they will explain the new policy and options for taking advantage of it.</u>

What's the Job? Legal secretaries are responsible for writing letters to clients or attorneys to pass on or obtain information. Read details of a letter that a legal secretary wrote to an attorney in another firm.

Activity 2 Read the letter. Then correct errors in pronoun use. You may have to completely rewrite one or more sentences.

Dear Mr. Templeton:

Mr. Brown received a copy of the divorce petition *Clark* v. *Clark*, which you filed on behalf of Mr. Clark, the plaintiff. You mentioned in your cover letter that Mr. Tim Grey will assist in representing Mr. Clark. We want to set up depositions in this case as soon as possible. He will need to be prepared with a list of personal items that they contest. The court clerk will require a copy as well, as they must file it with the petition. Please send a copy of it to Mr. Brown and I, so that we can be prepared for the meeting.

See page 121 for sample answers.

····Your Turn····

Use your own paper to write a response to the prompt on this page. When writing your response, remember to follow the writing process.

Prewrite: Generate and list your ideas about the topic. Then organize your ideas.

Draft: Write your draft using your ideas and your plan for organization. **Use pronouns with clear antecedents.**

Revise: Read your draft, looking for ways to improve it. **Rewrite sentences to make antecedents clear if necessary.**

Edit: Read your draft again, looking for errors in grammar, spelling, capitalization, and punctuation. **Make sure subject pronouns and object pronouns are used correctly. Check for agreement in number between pronoun and antecedent.**

Testing Tip

Often in a test response, a writer may use the personal pronoun *you* to refer to someone in general, as in "You can easily separate computer paper from other waste paper." The indefinite pronoun *one* may also be used: "One can easily separate computer paper from other waste paper." Either pronoun is correct, but choose one and use it consistently. Don't shift back and forth between *you* and *one*.

Prompt:

The Green Committee at work has asked for your ideas about how to improve recycling efforts in your workplace. The committee feels that too much paper is used and thrown away. In addition, recyclable cans and bottles are ending up in the regular trash.

Write a memo that explains your ideas for a recycling program in your workplace. Be specific and give reasons for your point of view.

KEY POINTS

When writing for business:

→ Identify whether a pronoun is a subject or an object, and use the correct pronoun.

→ Make sure the antecedent of a pronoun is clear.

→ Make sure the pronoun and its antecedent agree in number—both singular or both plural.

See page 121 for a sample response.

Using
Punctuation

KEYS TO...

Using Punctuation

When reading the lesson, keep the following points in mind:

→ Punctuation helps make writing clearer and easier to read.

→ Commas separate words and ideas in a sentence, but they are often not needed.

→ A semicolon separates the independent clauses in a compound sentence.

→ An apostrophe is used in possessives and contractions.

KEY Words

semicolon (;) mark used to separate two complete thoughts

apostrophe (') mark used in possessives and contractions For more about punctuation, see the Business Writer's Reference page 106.

WorkKeys® in REAL LIFE

Preschool teachers instruct children up to five years old in activities that help them grow intellectually, socially, and physically. Preschool teachers must keep records of each child and write reports and letters to parents. Punctuation helps make their writing easier to understand.

Electromechanical technicians operate, test, and maintain automated electromechanical equipment. Part of an electromechanical technician's job is to prepare written testing documentation, correctly punctuated.

The Skill

Without punctuation, the most carefully crafted business writing would be difficult to read. Punctuation helps group words and show how a writer's ideas relate to each other. The following uses of the **semicolon**, the comma, and the **apostrophe** are ones that often cause business writers problems:

- Use a semicolon to separate two complete thoughts, or independent clauses, in a compound sentence: *Jake can count to ten; he has also learned colors and shapes.*
- Use a comma *along with a conjunction* to separate two independent clauses in a compound sentence: *Jake can count to ten,* **and** *he has learned colors and shapes.*
- Use a comma to separate three or more items in a series: *The afternoon activities include story time, dress up, and art.*
- Do not use a comma to separate a compound subject or compound predicate: *The four-year-olds eat lunch at noon and then return to their room for a nap.* (no comma after *noon*)
- Use an apostrophe to show possession, *not* to form a plural: *Gia's exam revealed hearing loss, but the other girls' hearing is fine. The boys are due to be tested tomorrow.* (no apostrophe in *boys*)
- Use an apostrophe in a contraction: **It's** *important that the preschool keep* **its** *accreditation.* (an apostrophe in *it's—short* for *it is*; no apostrophe in the possessive *its*)

HERE'S HOW

What's the Job? Preschool teachers sometimes must write incident reports to parents, along with performing other assigned duties. Read part of the report that a preschool teacher wrote about an accident involving a child.

> Grace fell on the playground today, and she cut her left knee. ❶
> Our nurse cleaned, disinfected, and bandaged the wound ❷ ❷
> immediately. Grace cried for several minutes; however, she was ❸
> able to return to normal play in a short time. Our nurse's ❹
> phone number is 555—7078 if you have any questions or concerns.

❶ A comma is used with the conjunction *and* in this compound sentence.

❷ The commas help the reader distinguish items in a list.

❸ A semicolon is used in this compound sentence; note the comma after the subsequent word *however*.

❹ An apostrophe and *s* tell you that *nurse's* is a singular possessive noun.

To appreciate punctuation, read the first two sentences of the report without it: "Grace fell on the playground today and she cut her left knee Our nurse cleaned disinfected and bandaged the wound immediately"

Read the following note written by a preschool teacher. Then choose how the note should be edited so that punctuation is used correctly.

> Please do not forget that tomorrow is our school's field trip to
> the county zoo. The bus will leave at 9:00 so your child needs to
> be here no later than 8:30. We'll stay at the zoo until 12:00;
> pickup is at the regular dismissal time. Each child should bring a
> snack, a jacket, and the attached permission form, signed.

A. Remove the apostrophe in *school's*.
B. Insert a comma after *9:00*.
C. Change the semicolon after *12:00* to a comma.

What Do I Need to Know? Look carefully at each punctuation mark. Ask what rule applies to its use.

- Option A is incorrect. The apostrophe in *school's* is needed because the word is possessive.
- Option C is incorrect. The semicolon correctly separates two independent clauses without a coordinating conjunction.
- Option B is correct. A comma should be inserted to separate two independent clauses joined by the conjunction *so*. The answer is *B—Insert a comma after* 9:00.

> **KEYS** *to Success*
>
> A semicolon can be a good way to achieve sentence variety in your writing.

Try It

Use a sheet of paper for these writing activities.

Activity 1 Refer to page 106 for other uses of the comma. Then rewrite each memo, correcting the errors in punctuation. Some errors are the overuse of punctuation.

Activity 1 Refer to page 106 for other uses of the comma. Then rewrite each memo, correcting the errors in punctuation. Some errors are the overuse of punctuation.

1. Customer Marianna Hannigan called to report a problem with the zoom function on her Ninsa XC45 camera. She said that it's zoom was working fine until yesterday. I followed protocol A by asking her to turn off the camera, and press the "check battery" light. When she stated that the red light was on; I informed her that she should charge the battery overnight.

2. Every floor worker, and every supervisor will be asked to work overtime this weekend to take inventory. Please make an effort to get here on time so that we can leave at a reasonable hour each day. Wear casual comfortable, and cool clothes we will be moving around a lot. Ill be at the front office signing people in, and Nick Burns will be in the back assigning jobs. Let's work together; the more efficient we are, the sooner the job will get done!

What's the Job? An electromechanical technician writes detailed reports after he or she has tested a piece of equipment. The report below is an account of some recent testing.

Activity 2 Read the report. Then copy it, inserting commas, semicolons, and apostrophes where they belong.

> **ATTN: VIKING 457 SUPPORT TEAM**
>
> My team conducted these three quality control tests on the Viking 457: an electrical power summary a complete computer update assessment and an emergency response test. All three tests were completed within the required 8-hour period and all three tests indicated 100% satisfactory performance of this equipment. We also ran a complete system check twice during the next 8 hours this check was performed to ensure reliability. Were pleased to report that the Viking 457 is running at excellent efficiency.

See page 121 for sample answers.

Your Turn

Use your own paper to write a response to the prompt on this page. When writing your response, remember to follow the writing process.

Prewrite: Generate and list your ideas about the topic. Then organize your ideas.

Draft: Write your draft using your ideas and your plan for organization.

Revise: Read your draft, looking for ways to improve it.

Edit: Read your draft again, looking for errors in grammar, spelling, capitalization, and punctuation. **Make sure you have used commas, semicolons, apostrophes, and other punctuation marks correctly, including not overusing them.**

Prompt:

The human resources department where you work is reviewing its current maternity and paternity leave policy. State law mandates at least 6 weeks of paid leave, but some companies offer more than this, on either a paid or an unpaid basis.

Write a letter to the department explaining your point of view on maternity and paternity leave. Give reasons for your opinions.

KEYS to Success

Traditionally, contractions were considered informal language and inappropriate for formal business writing. Modern usage has become less formal, and their limited use is now acceptable in standard business English.

Testing Tip

Allow about 5 minutes to review your response and edit it for punctuation and other errors in mechanics. Small errors in punctuation can affect the readability of your writing and therefore your score.

KEY POINTS

When writing for business:

→ Punctuation helps make writing more readable.

→ Use a semicolon to separate two complete thoughts that are not linked by a conjunction.

→ Use a comma before a conjunction that separates two complete thoughts and to separate three or more items in a series.

→ Do not overuse commas.

→ Use an apostrophe in possessives and contractions.

See pages 121–122 for a sample response.

Spelling
Correctly

KEYS TO...

Spelling Correctly

When reading the lesson, keep the following points in mind:

→ Have a dictionary on hand whenever you are writing on the job and use it.

→ Focus on words you often misspell.

→ Pay particular attention to commonly misspelled words such as homonyms and contractions.

→ Learn spelling rules.

WorkKeys® in REAL LIFE

Store department managers supervise retail salespeople. They deal with both employees and customers every day. Solid communication skills, including knowledge of grammar and spelling, are essential in their work.

Typists and word processors type letters, reports, and other documents from rough drafts written by others. These workers must pay attention to detail. Often, typists and word processors identify and fix spelling and grammar errors in the documents they are typing.

The Skill

Have you ever read a piece of writing that contains numerous spelling errors? Most people find these mistakes distracting. Misspelled words make writing harder to understand, and they reflect poorly on the writer.

Successful business writers do a number of things to improve their spelling skills: (1) They use a good dictionary—either print or online—and take the time to look up the spelling of words they are unsure of. (2) They tackle their own "spelling demons," or words they tend to misspell, by keeping a record of the words and learning their correct spelling. (3) They remember useful spelling tips, such as those below.

- **Homophones** are words that sound the same but are spelled differently. Be careful to choose the spelling that matches your meaning. Some commonly confused homophones are *there* (location), *their* (possession), and *they're* ("they are"); *to* (preposition), *two* (2), and *too* ("also"); *your* (possession) and *you're* ("you are"); *hear* (listen) and *here* (location).

- Remember spelling rules such as "*i* before *e* except after *c* or when sounded as "ay" as in *neighbor* and *weigh*. Common business words following this rule are *receive*, *receipt*, and *chief*.

- Add **suffixes** and other endings to words correctly. Sometimes the spelling of the base word changes: *judge* + *-ment* = *judgment*; *begin* + *-ing* = *beginning*; *manage* + *-ing* = *managing*; *factory* + *-es* = *factories*. Also, similar-sounding syllables may have different spellings: *occur**rence***, *insur**ance***; *collect**ible***, *pay**able***.

KEY Words

homophones words that sound the same but are spelled differently. See page 103 for some problem homophones.

suffixes groups of letters added to the end of a word

HERE'S HOW

What's the Job? Store department managers sometimes leave messages for other store personnel regarding customer purchases, orders, and comments. Good spelling is important because it makes reading easier and looks more professional. Read this note and pay attention to how the writer applied the spelling tips.

> Two deliveries will be arriving tomorrow from Chef Plus, ❶ ❷ ❷
> Inc. Please set order #81065 aside for Mrs. Lisa Fay, who
> will pick it up Friday. She has paid in full, and she will bring her
> receipt. You're welcome to shelve the other order on the ❸ ❹
> kitchen aids shelf if your time allows.

❶ The homophone *two* (2) and the contraction *you're* ("you are") are the correct spellings in these contexts.

❷ The endings were added correctly to *delivery* (change the *y* to *i* and add *-es*) and *arrive* (drop the final silent *-e* before adding *-ing*).

❸ The *e* comes before the *i* when *c* precedes in the word *receipt*.

Imagine the impression this note would make if the highlighted words had been misspelled.

Read the following details of a message regarding a customer request. Which word is misspelled?

> John Simmons called again this morning, seeking information
> regarding the hockey equipment he ordered several weeks ago.
> This merchandise should have been hear on September 2. I believe
> Don is the contact person for this supplier. Can someone call Don
> before it is too late to accommodate this customer?

A. equipment
B. hear
C. believe
D. supplier
E. too

What Do I Need to Know? Look at each word, applying the spelling tips.

- Option A: The spelling of *equip* doesn't change when *-ment* is added.
- Option B: The homophone in this context means "in this place."
- Option C: *Believe* is spelled correctly; *i* comes before *e* unless preceded by *c*.
- Option D: The spelling of the base word *supply* must change when *-er* is added. Change *y* to *i* before adding the suffix.
- Option E: This is the correct homophone: *too* means "also."
- The answer is *B—hear*.

KEYS *to Success*

You cannot always rely on the spell-check function on your computer. It cannot distinguish between homophones.

Try It

Activity 1 Write the word in parentheses that is correctly spelled for the context.

1. Order #092386 will be delayed for (to, two, too) more weeks. Please call Mrs. Hughes and let her (no, know) that the shipment will be (comming, coming) late.

2. We (beleive, believe) that it (would, wood) be (advisable, adviseable) to draft a (new, knew) list of rules and (regulations, regulateions).

3. (Its, It's) difficult to understand how our (employee's, employees) could ignore basic safety standards. Yet many continue to refuse to (where, wear) the required vests and goggles provided (for, four) them.

4. Mr. Angeles would like to know (weather, whether) you and (your, you're) department will be (attending, attendding) Tuesday's staff meeting.

What's the Job? Typists and word processors take rough drafts written by other employees and input them neatly and accurately into a computer file or onto paper. They need to check for accurate spelling as they work. Just because someone wrote a word in one way does not mean it is correct.

Activity 2 Read the letter. Then copy it, correcting the spelling mistakes.

Dear Mr. DeVry:

I am righting this letter to inform you that your account is past due for the second month. There are to ways to take care of this problem. Here are your options:

First, you can pay the outstandding balance by credit card.

Second, you can call hour credit department to make arrangments for a payment plan.

Please call us to confirm that you have recieved this letter. If you ignore this notice, you risk becomming a discreditted customer. If this were too happen, you would no longer be able to place you're orders via the Internet or phone. All your orders would have to be payed for in cash only.

Your Turn

Use your own paper to write a response to the prompt on this page. When writing your response, remember to follow the writing process.

Prewrite: Generate and list your ideas about the topic. Figure out what your main idea is. Then organize your ideas.

Draft: Write your draft using your ideas and your plan for organization.

Revise: Read your draft, looking for ways to improve it.

Edit: Read your draft again, **looking for errors in spelling**, grammar, capitalization, and punctuation. **Pay particular attention to homophones, words with suffixes, and your personal spelling demons.**

Testing Tip

If you are taking the writing test on paper and notice a misspelling, it is acceptable to cross out the misspelled word and write the correct spelling above it. That will not count against your score.

Prompt:

The company you work for has had a longstanding policy prohibiting personal Internet use during work hours. Some employees have requested that this policy be changed, citing their need to access information that is available only via the computer. They ask that rules for the Internet be similar to those for the telephone.

Write a memo explaining what you think the workplace Internet usage rules should be. Give reasons for your ideas.

KEY POINTS

When writing for business:

➔ Keep a dictionary on hand and use it.

➔ Tackle your spelling demons.

➔ Learn spelling rules.

➔ Pay attention to homophones and words with suffixes and other endings.

➔ Always edit your document for spelling.

See page 122 for a sample response.

Using
Capitalization

WorkKeys® in REAL LIFE

Curriculum coordinators develop teaching materials and programs for training teachers. They prepare curricula recommendations for school systems. Their work requires writing documents that are clear and free from errors, including mistakes in capitalization.

Medical secretaries answer phones, schedule patient visits, and interview patients. They also write letters to patients, insurance companies, or other medical professionals. Their writing must be error-free, including capitalization mistakes, to maintain the confidence of others.

The Skill

Good business writers pay attention to details that give their writing a polished finish, which makes an impression on coworkers, supervisors, clients, and customers. One of those details is correct capitalization.

Here are a few rules of capitalization that apply particularly to business writing. As with punctuation, overuse of capitalization is just as much an error as not capitalizing terms that should be capitalized:

- Capitalize a title when it precedes the person's name or follows it on an address or signature line: *Chairman Andrews; John Andrew, Chairman; Vice-President of Finance, Peter Epstein.*
- Do not capitalize a title when it is apart from the name or used in place of the name: *The president of the company will give a speech.*
- Capitalize the names of companies, corporations, and other businesses: *Hallmark Engineering, Presbyterian Hospital.*
- Capitalize many acronyms. An **acronym** is an abbreviation that consists of the initial letters of the full name: *CEO (Chief Executive Officer).*
- Rules for capitalizing words associated with the Internet are not settled. Most dictionaries capitalize *Internet*, *World Wide Web*, and *Web site*. Other publications, such as those by Microsoft, use lowercase letters. For now, the important thing in a business document is consistency. Decide to capitalize these terms or not, and use the same format throughout.
- For more capitalization rules, see the Business Writer's Reference page 107.

KEY Words

acronym   an abbreviation consisting of the initial letters of a phrase; sometimes an acronym is read as a word rather than individual letters.

HERE'S HOW

What's the Job? Curriculum coordinators are responsible for writing letters, memos, and reports. Read part of a letter that a curriculum coordinator wrote to a school superintendent.

Dr. James Thurman, Superintendent ❶
Middleton School District

Dear Dr. Thurman:

Dr. Thornton, the chairman of my committee, suggested I write to set ❷ up a meeting to discuss the technical classes you offer in your schools. Thursday would be good for me if you are available,

I will be traveling throughout the state to meet with district supervisors ❷ to review their curricula related to new technologies. I also have found some helpful Web sites on the Internet. ❸

❶ Titles that are used in an address or signature line are always capitalized.

❷ Titles that act as a description following a person's name, or that do not refer to a specific person, are not capitalized.

❸ Be consistent in whether you do or do not capitalize words related to the Internet.

Read the following memo. Then choose the sentence showing the appropriate correction in capitalization.

Angela Thompson, the director of language arts at Grant College, has asked for our help. She wants to incorporate technology in her English composition courses. I plan to meet with her and professor Marcos later this week.

A. Angela Thompson, the Director of Language Arts at Grant College, has asked for our help.

B. She wants to incorporate Technology in her English composition courses.

C. I plan to meet with her and Professor Marcos later this week.

What Do I Need to Know? Look at each sentence, applying the rules of capitalization.

- In option A, the title *director of language arts* occurs after the name within a sentence, so it should not be capitalized.

- In option B, the word *technology* need not be capitalized.

- In option C, the title *professor* occurs before the name, so it should be capitalized. The answer is *C—I plan to meet with her and Professor Marcos later this week.*

Try It

Use a sheet of paper for these writing activities.

Activity 1 Refer to page 107 for capitalization rules. Then read each memo. Write *OK* if the underlined sentence contains no capitalization errors. If there is an error in the sentence, rewrite it, correcting the error.

1. <u>We need to do more to develop the sports programs at Evans High School.</u> Most of the Evans Grizzlies teams are for boys only. Except for the basketball program, there are very few programs in which girls participate. I agree with Coach Barker that we need to expand the program.

2. Dr. Jordan Hamilton, professor of neuroscience at the University of Michigan, has agreed to review the section on the brain in our new science textbook. <u>Since professor Hamilton is one of the most renowned scientists in the field of neuroscience, we believe this will guarantee the accuracy of this complex subject.</u> I plan to get the manuscripts to the professor right away.

3. Construction on the Wainwright Federal Building was approved by the zoning board. <u>Without the help of Congressman Johnston, the project would not have been approved by the president.</u> The next step is to take bids from construction companies capable of completing this project on time and at cost.

What's the Job? Medical secretaries write memos and letters to patients and to other medical professionals. The following memo was written to patients by a medical secretary.

Activity 2 Read the memo. Then rewrite it, correcting errors in capitalization.

> **TO: PATIENTS OF DR. MENDOZA:**
> We will be moving our offices from 212 Mercy Drive to 1710 Clinton Drive. This move will be effective on monday, December 12. While we realize that this is a big move for many of you, dr. Mendoza feels that we can provide better service from this location. Our old offices in the North section of the City have been updated several times over the years, but our new offices will be in a brand new Medical Building farther south, near the intersection of Rice street and Lake drive. If you have any questions about our move, you can call us or visit our web site on the Internet.

See page 122 for sample answers.

Your Turn

Use your own paper to write a response to the prompt on this page. When writing your response, remember to follow the writing process.

Prewrite: Generate and list your ideas about the topic. Then organize your ideas.

Draft: Write your draft using your ideas and your plan for organization.

Revise: Read your draft, looking for ways to improve it.

Edit: Read your draft again, **looking for errors in capitalization**, grammar, spelling, and punctuation. **Correct any mistakes in capitalization you find.**

Testing Tip

Read through the writing prompt slowly and carefully. Think about what proper names and titles you may use in the response.

Prompt:

Because your company has a no-smoking policy in and around its buildings, workers now have to travel quite a distance to smoke a cigarette. Management has noticed that, as a result, smoking breaks have lengthened from five minutes to fifteen or twenty minutes. Some nonsmokers have complained that they are not getting equal treatment since their breaks are still five minutes.

Write a letter to company management to explain how you think this issue should be addressed.

KEY POINTS

When writing for business:

➜ Recognize the importance of capitalizing correctly.

➜ Follow the rules of capitalization.

➜ Be consistent in capitalizing terms related to the Internet.

➜ Edit your writing for correct capitalization.

See page 122 for a sample response.

GOING FOR THE GOLD For the Unit 5 Assessment and the online Posttest, go to www.mysteckvaughn.com/CAREER.

Common Errors that Business Writers Make

When you write, try to avoid making these errors. When you revise and edit, look for them in order to improve and correct your writing.

Development of Ideas

➔ Making simple, obvious statements

➔ Merely repeating statements

➔ Making overly general, unsupported statements

Organization

➔ Lacking a clear focus or central message

➔ Random ordering of ideas

➔ Incorrect, simple, or no transitions:
The ideas were interesting and the evidence was skimpy.

Style and Tone

➔ Rude diction:
That report stinks. Don't waste my time with it.

➔ Slang or informal diction:
She is an awesome worker.

Sentence Structure

➔ Fragment:
A team member always willing to help others.

➔ Run-on:
Shawn is a careful forklift operator he follows all the safety rules.

➔ Comma splice:
She worked overtime, she completed the project on time.

Grammar, Usage, and Mechanics

➔ Wrong verb tense:
They make the hotel arrangements yesterday.

➔ Shifting tense:
He marked down the prices but forgets to enter them into the computer.

➔ Incorrect subject-verb agreement:
The employees wants more challenge.

➔ Unclear pronoun antecedent:
I work with Gloria and Jean and find her more flexible.

➔ Missing word or words:
The secretary's responsibility the memo.

➔ Misspellings:
We did not recieve the package on time.

➔ Incorrect or lack of punctuation:
The test was faulty, and should be repeated.

➔ Incorrect capitalization:
Marty worked late all Week and even on saturday.

Commonly Confused Words

Words	Definitions	Sentences
accept (*v.*)	to take something offered	Will she accept a transfer to another department?
except (*prep.*)	excluding	Except for the conclusion, the report was clear.
access (*n.*)	admittance	She has access to the company's president.
assess (*v.*)	to evaluate	Please assess the strengths of our new product.
affect (*v.*)	to influence	Her enthusiasm affected productivity.
effect (*n.* or *v.*)	result; to cause or bring about.	The manager's work ethic has a positive effect on his team. The director wants to effect sweeping changes.
already (*adv.*)	previously or by this time	The manager already approved the proposal.
all ready (*adj.*)	totally prepared	The team is all ready to discuss the budget.
altogether (*adv.*)	completely; on the whole	Altogether our company had a very good year.
all together (*adj.*)	with everybody or everything together at the same time	The employees eat all together in the cafeteria.
fewer (*adj.*)	not so many (used for things that can be counted)	Our staff has fewer sick days this year than last year.
less (*adj.*)	a smaller amount (used for quantities)	We have less time to complete the restocking.
its (*possessive pronoun*)	belonging to it	Our sales force is proud of its achievement awards.
it's (*contraction*)	it is	It's difficult to determine why sales declined.
principal (*adj.*)	main or chief	Our principal goal this quarter is to trim expenses.
principle (*n.*)	rule or belief	Her guiding principle is that hard work pays off.
respectfully (*adv.*)	in a way that shows respect	He respectfully declined the offer.
respectively (*adv.*)	each one in the order mentioned	Day and night shifts were Lou and Joe, respectively.
whether (*conj.*)	if	He does not know whether he will receive a promotion.
weather (*n.*)	atmospheric conditions	We expect mild weather for the company picnic.

Grammar and Usage Rules

Subject-Verb Agreement

→ The number of the subject—singular or plural—determines the number of the verb.

His job <u>performance</u> <u>impresses</u> his boss.

The <u>reports</u> <u>present</u> sales for the last two years.

→ Use a plural verb with a compound subject containing two or more nouns connected by *and*.

The <u>supervisor</u> and her <u>assistant</u> <u>work</u> well together.

→ Use a singular verb when two or more singular nouns are connected by *or* or *nor*.

<u>Monday</u> or <u>Friday</u> <u>is</u> a good day to telecommute.

Neither <u>Tuesday</u> nor <u>Thursday</u> <u>is</u> busy.

→ When a compound subject contains both a singular and a plural noun joined by *or* or *nor*, make the verb agree with the noun that is closer to it.

The board members or the <u>president</u> <u>has</u> the authority to sign.

→ Make sure the verb agrees with the subject when a phrase comes between the two.

<u>Each</u> of the employees <u>contributes</u> to a retirement savings plan.

→ Collective nouns are singular in form but name a group, such as *audience*, *committee*, *herd*, *crowd*, and *family*. Use a singular verb when a collective noun refers to the group as a whole acting together.

The committee <u>meets</u> on Monday morning.

→ Use a plural verb when a collective noun refers to individual members acting separately.

The committee <u>vote</u> on policy changes.

→ Indefinite pronouns include such words as *anyone*, *none*, and *something*. Use a singular verb with any indefinite pronoun ending in *–one*, *–body*, and *–thing*.

<u>Everybody</u> <u>earns</u> comp time.

→ Always use a singular verb with the indefinite pronouns *another*, *each*, *either*, *neither*, and *one*.

Both products are reliable; <u>either</u> is a good choice.

Verb Forms and Irregular Verbs

Verbs have four principal parts: the present, present participle, simple past, and past participle. Regular verbs form the simple past and the past participle by adding *–d* or *–ed* to the present. Participles require auxiliary, or helping, verbs (*am working*; *have shipped*; *had bought*).

Present	Present Participle	Simple Past	Past Participle
work	working	worked	worked
ship	shipping	shipped	shipped
create	creating	created	created

Irregular verbs form the simple past and past participle in different ways.

Present	Present Participle	Simple Past	Past Participle
become	becoming	became	become
begin	beginning	began	begun
bring	bringing	brought	brought
buy	buying	bought	bought
choose	choosing	chose	chosen
come	coming	came	come
get	getting	got	got, gotten
know	knowing	knew	known
lead	leading	led	led
see	seeing	saw	seen
speak	speaking	spoke	spoken
take	taking	took	taken
tell	telling	told	told
think	thinking	thought	thought
write	writing	wrote	written

The most commonly used auxiliary verbs are forms of the verbs *be* (*am, is, being, was, were, been*) and *have* (*has, having, had, have*). These verbs are used with a main verb to express different tenses.

Verb Tenses

Verb tenses indicate the time of an action or a state of being: the past, the present, or the future. The principal parts of the verb are used to form various tenses:

→ Present tense:

The clinic sees many patients every day.

→ Past tense:

The clinic saw many patients last month.

→ Future tense:

The clinic will see many patients this month.

→ Present perfect tense:

The clinic has seen more patients this month than last.

→ Past perfect tense:

The clinic had seen many patients before it closed.

→ Future perfect tense:

The clinic will have seen many patients by the end of the week.

Verbs also have the following forms:

→ Progressive form:

The clinic is seeing more patients these days.
The clinic was seeing fewer patients when it closed.

→ Emphatic forms:

The clinic does see a great many patients.
The clinic did see a great many patients.

Keep verbs in the same tense when two or more events occur at the same time. Change tenses only to show that one event occurred before or after another.

Todd sold the equipment and notified his supervisor.

Before the customer called, I already had sold the last book.

Pronouns

Pronouns replace nouns (their antecedents), taking different forms depending on their function in a sentence. Subject pronouns are used as subjects, object pronouns are used as objects, and possessive pronouns show possession. Reflexive pronouns are used as objects when the object and subject are the same (*A worker hurt himself on the lathe.*). An intensive pronoun follows its antecedent, emphasizing it (*The CEO himself handed out awards at the dinner.*).

	Subject	Object	Possessive	Reflexive/Intensive
1st person	I, we	me	my, mine	myself
		us	our, ours	ourselves
2nd person	you	you	your, yours	yourself
3rd person	he, she, it	him, her, it	his, her, hers, its	himself, herself, itself, themselves
	they	them	their, theirs	

Pronouns agree with their antecedents in number (singular or plural), gender (masculine, feminine, or neuter), and person (first, second, or third person):

Because Sophia worked diligently on the project, the CEO awarded her.

(The pronoun *her* is singular, feminine, and third person.)

The company reported its profits.

(The pronoun *its* is singular, neuter, and third person.)

The managers praised their staffs.

(The pronoun *their* is plural and third person.)

Indefinite pronouns do not refer to specific persons or things. Some indefinite pronouns are singular, such as *anyone, each, everything, no one,* and *some one.* The indefinite pronouns *both, many, few,* and *several* are plural. The indefinite pronouns *all, some, any,* and *none* may be either singular or plural, depending on their meaning in a sentence.

All of the report is true.
None of the reports are dull.

Punctuation Rules

Commas

The comma groups words that belong together and signals a momentary pause.

→ Place a comma before a coordinating conjunction (*and*, *but*, *or*, *nor*, *for*, so, and *yet*) that joins two independent clauses in a compound sentence.

The order was shipped five days ago, but it has not arrived yet.

→ Use a comma to separate an introductory phrase or subordinate clause from the rest of the sentence.

Even though our schedule is demanding, our team will meet it.

For us to meet this schedule, overtime will be necessary.

→ Use commas to separate items in a series or list.

The departments located on this site are marketing, sales, editorial, and design.

→ Use a comma to set off nonrestrictive (additional but not essential) information.

Linda Brown, a sales associate, has been promoted to department manager.

→ Use a comma after the closing of a business letter. Use a comma to separate a name from a title following it.

With regards,
Marcus Johnson, President

→ Use a comma to separate elements of addresses and dates.

Please send two copies of the contract to 8400 Mesa Dr., Albuquerque, NM 87120, postdated no later than January 26, 2011.

Colons

→ Use a colon to introduce a list. Note that the colon should not come directly after a verb.

Our company respects and rewards the following qualities in our employees: enthusiasm, effort, and commitment.

→ Use a colon to introduce a formal statement.

We embraces this principle: the right of every employee to realize his or her potential.

→ Use a colon after the greeting, or salutation, in a business letter.

Dear Mr. Blake:

→ Use a colon in times.

8:30 A.M.

Apostrophes

→ Use an apostrophe and an *s* to form the possessive of a singular noun and of a plural noun that does not end in *s*.

the company's president
the women's luncheon

→ Use only an apostrophe to form the possessive of a plural noun that ends in *s*.

competitors' products

→ Use an apostrophe and an *s* to form the plural of a letter or a word used as a word.

cross the *i*'s and dot the *t*'s
all those *thank you*'s

→ Use an apostrophe to form a contraction.

it is = it's

Capitalization Rules

1. Capitalize the first word of a sentence.

   Employers use job interviews to identify the most qualified candidates.

2. Capitalize the names of persons, academic degrees, and titles.

Nathan S. Moore	Chad Forman, Ph.D
Dr. Mafat Patel	Ms. Inez Baca
Diane Smoltz, President	President Diane Smoltz

   Do not capitalize a title when it occurs apart from the name in a sentence.

   The president of our company is Diane Smoltz.

3. Capitalize the names of days, months, and holidays, but not seasons.

Sunday	March
Memorial Day	summer

4. Capitalize the names of organizations, businesses, corporations, products, institutions, and government agencies. Capitalize abbreviations that are part of those names.

   Chicago Food Depository
   Newberry Library

   Orosco Landscaping Company
   Department of Labor

   Bryce Corporation
   Merrihill, Inc.

   Colonel Bingham's Popcorn
   Regis Co., Ltd.

5. Capitalize place names, regions, and street names, including abbreviations.

Denver, Colorado	Central Street
India	Lake Shore Drive
West Coast	Southern Blvd.

6. Capitalize the names of nationalities, historical and cultural events, and religions.

Chinese	Hispanic Heritage Month
Vietnam War	Islam

7. Capitalize many acronyms (abbreviations that consist of the initial letters of the full name).

   CEO (Chief Executive Officer)

   CFO (Chief Financial Officer)

   OSHA (Occupational Safety and Health Administration)

8. Capitalize the inside address, salutation, and closing of a letter.

   Marianna Rogers, Dean of Faculty
   Genoese College
   Wilmington, Vermont

   Dear Dean Rogers:

   Sincerely yours,

9. Capitalize the names of continents, bodies of water, and landforms.

   North America

   Pacific Ocean

   Rocky Mountains

10. Capitalize the first word, the last word, and all important words in the titles of books and films.

    What Color Is Your Parachute?

    After the Axe

Career Advice

The famed Chinese teacher and philosopher Confucius said, "Choose a job you love, and you will never have to work a day in your life." The act of choosing a job can be a complicated task, however. A job seeker must assess his or her skills, experiences, and interests and then match them with the demands of the job market. As is true of all complex tasks, a successful job search is dependent on a series of steps.

STEP 1 Assess Your WorkKeys® Skills

Review the results of your *CareerReady*™ Posttest and use those results to identify areas that require further study. Then, review the specific lessons that teach those skills. If necessary, ask your instructor for additional help with any skills that you have not yet mastered.

STEP 2 Research Occupational Information

The next step is to research potential occupations that match your skills, experience, and interests. There are several online resources available to you:

→ ACT's online job profile database contains an alphabetized list of job titles and their associated WorkKeys® skill levels. Search for jobs that interest you and that match your skill levels.

→ O*Net® Online has information about the job titles you will find on the ACT job profile database. This Web site includes job descriptions, required training, salary information, and more.

→ The Bureau of Labor Statistics Web site and the Occupational Outlook Handbook have more information about specific job titles. These resources are updated regularly with job outlook and projections data for specific jobs and occupational groups.

STEP 3 Use Job-Hunting Resources

Once you have identified potential jobs that match your skills, experience, and interests, the next step is to locate actual job openings. Job-hunting in the twenty-first century requires a nimble mind and an Internet connection. Based on the popularity and ease-of-use of the Internet, many companies post current lists of job openings on their company Web sites or on sites such as Monster or CareerBuilder. The U.S. Department of Labor offers State Job Banks that highlight public and private job openings. Additionally, you can search USAJobs for public service, local, regional, and national information for federal careers.

Although job openings may be relatively easy to find, it is not enough to submit your résumé and hope for the best. Keep in mind that the hiring process is ultimately based on personal contact with the people who have the power to hire you—in other words, networking.

STEP 4 Use Effective Interviewing Strategies

You have browsed job openings, submitted résumés, and made use of your personal and professional network. Your hard work has paid off, and you have been chosen for an interview. However, an interview is not a job guarantee. Surpass your competition by following these ten strategies:

1. Display knowledge about the industry and the prospective employer's role in the industry. You can find detailed information about a company through the company Web site, search engines, and local newspapers.

2. Determine how your skills, experience, and interests apply to the job you seek. Be prepared to talk about how you can use your current skills and knowledge within the context of this new job.

3. Prepare and practice a thirty-second speech that highlights your skills and experience and shows how you will help the company accomplish its goals.

4. Analyze the job description and write a list of questions for the interviewer. This preparation shows that you have taken the time to consider the position and your suitability for it.

5. Write a list of questions about the company. Make sure the answers to your questions cannot be found on the company Web site.

6. Verify beforehand that you know how to find the location of the interview and arrive early for your interview.

7. Dress in a professional manner.

8. Provide the interviewer with copies of relevant documents, such as your résumé, identification, portfolio, or school or college transcripts.

9. Maintain eye contact with the interviewer. Use proper pacing and expression. Focus on how you can help the company, not on how the company can help you.

10. Make sure to follow up after the interview by sending a handwritten thank-you note or an e-mail to your interviewer. Thank him or her for the interview, summarize the high points of the discussion, and reaffirm your interest in the job opening.

STEP 5 Pay Attention to Job Market Trends

The following list from the U.S. Department of Labor, Bureau of Labor Statistics, shows the thirty jobs with the largest projected employment growth over the next several years. You can cross-reference most of the jobs on this list with the ACT online job profile database to learn the related WorkKeys® skill levels. For example, on average, a registered nurse needs the following skill levels: Reading for Information, 5; Applied Mathematics, 4; Locating Information, 4; Business Writing, 4.

Occupations			
1	Registered Nurses	16	Administrative Assistants
2	Healthcare Support Workers	17	Management Analysts
3	Customer Service Representatives	18	Computer Software Engineers
4	Food Preparation and Serving Related Workers	19	Receptionists and Information Clerks
5	Personal and Home Care Aides	20	Carpenter Assemblers and Repairers
6	Retail Salespersons	21	Medical Assistants
7	Office Clerks	22	First-line and Office Supervisors/Managers
8	Accountants or Auditors	23	Database Administrators
9	Nursing Aides, Orderlies, and Attendants	24	Licensed Practical and Vocational Nurses
10	Postsecondary Teachers	25	Security Guards
11	Construction and Related Workers	26	Waiters and Waitresses
12	Elementary School Teachers	27	General Maintenance and Repair Workers
13	Truck Drivers	28	Physicians and Surgeons
14	Landscaping and Groundskeeping Workers	29	Child Care Workers
15	Bookkeeper Clerks	30	Teacher Assistants

Source: United States Department of Labor/Bureau of Labor Statistics

Peer Review Checklist

Ask a peer to review your response to a prompt. Have the reviewer complete this checklist to show whether your response met each criterion.

	YES	NO
Development of Ideas		
Is the main idea of the writing clear?		
Does each paragraph contain a topic sentence?		
Do enough details support each topic sentence?		
Are any ideas merely repeated?		
Are any unnecessary ideas included?		
Organization		
Are the details written in a logical order?		
Is there a clear introduction?		
Is there an effective conclusion?		
Do transitions help lead from idea to idea?		
Style and Tone		
Does the writing sound professional and courteous?		
Are the ideas clearly expressed?		
Are words precise and vivid?		
Do some words occur too many times?		
Is there slang or informal language?		
Sentence Structure		
Are all sentences complete?		
Are any sentences long and rambling?		
Are any sentences short and choppy?		
Do sentences vary in length?		
Do sentences vary in structure?		
Are there various sentence openings?		
Grammar, Usage, and Mechanics		
Do all the verbs agree with their subjects?		
Are verb forms used correctly?		
Are verb tenses correct and consistent?		
Is the punctuation correct in every sentence?		
Are all words spelled correctly?		
Is the capitalization correct in every sentence?		

Overall, on a scale of 1 to 5, how would you rate this response? _____

Answers and Responses

Pretest (p. 1)

Model Level 5 Response:

For instructor evaluation, use the rubric on page vi.

Cutting a lunch hour in half would be questionable for any reason. To cut it in half just to benefit the company cafeteria and the employees who patronize it is unwise and unfair. Rather than make the majority of employees adapt to the needs of the cafeteria, it makes more sense for the cafeteria to adapt to the needs of the employees.

Employees begin work at 7:30. By noon, they are tired and hungry and need a break, both physically and mentally. Leaving the company premises can help rejuvenate them. Certainly, too, the variety of restaurant choices in the area makes the lunch hour more enjoyable. It helps make each day a little different. Employees return to work by 1:00 refreshed and alert and ready for an afternoon of work.

In contrast, a half hour does not allow enough time for employees to go out to restaurants, enjoy a good lunch, or perhaps even do a little shopping. In fact, a half hour is not adequate time to relax and refresh even in the company cafeteria. The result will be employees returning to work still tired, still needing a break. What wisdom is there in that? A half hour lunch in effect forces employees to subsidize the cafeteria. How fair is that?

If waste is an issue in the cafeteria because of declining numbers of employees eating there, then cafeteria management can adjust the amounts of food bought and cooked. Employees who eat in the cafeteria may be paying higher prices than they used to, but the cost of meals in the cafeteria is still less than in local restaurants. Employees who want to go out for lunch but don't have transportation can always share a ride with coworkers. In fact, the time spent together at lunch might foster a greater feeling of belonging and stronger teamwork.

Where employees eat should be a matter of choice—their choice. If the company wants to continue its generally wise and fair policies, it will continue giving employees a full hour for lunch.

Lesson 1 Try It (p. 12)

Activity 1

1. OK

2. Forklift drivers should follow certain rules to improve safety.

3. We may have a temporary problem with acquiring tiles from Southwest Tile.

Activity 2

Our Employee Appreciation Picnic will be held this Saturday.

Lesson 1 Your Turn (p. 13)

For instructor evaluation, use the rubric on p. vi. For student evaluation, use the Peer Review Checklist on p. 111.

Model Level 5 Response:

More and more companies are thinking of new ways to help make their employees more productive, and telecommuting from home is certainly one way to accomplish this. While some may feel it is unfair that only certain office workers can take advantage of working at home, the benefits to the employee, our company, and even our city take precedence over the inequality of this opportunity.

For the telecommuting employee, working at home offers a degree of freedom. It means not wasting time, energy, and money going back and forth to the workplace, whether you drive or take public transportation. Your workplace is just steps away. In addition, it is easier to concentrate at home—free from distractions such as office phones ringing and coworkers chatting. More time and fewer distractions also add up to more stress-free conditions.

For our company, the benefits of allowing employees to telecommute are monetary. Time is money. Time spent behind the wheel of a car or looking out a commuter train window is not time spent working. In addition, the undistracted worker at home is far more productive. This increase in productivity created by telecommuting translates into higher profits for our company.

For the city, telecommuting offers great environmental benefits. The fuel used and the pollution caused by commuters in cars, buses, and trains are certainly major environmental concerns. Traffic jams during rush hour make a major carbon footprint. They even lead to road rage. Our company would be contributing to a greener community by allowing telecommuting.

It's clear to see the benefits of allowing those employees who can work at home to telecommute. When productivity and profits increase and pollution decreases, telecommuting makes smart policy.

Lesson 2 Try It (p. 16)

Activity 1

1. A traveling exhibit, "Abraham Lincoln: the Self-Reliant Leader," will be on display at the Glenmore Public Library. The exhibit features artifacts from Lincoln's life—such as his high hat—and the Civil War. The exhibit runs from October 14 until November 6. All are invited to tour it for free during the library's regular hours.

2. Intellectual freedom is the theme of Banned Books Week at the Glenmore Public Library. During the week the library will focus on the benefits of free access to information and the harm of censorship. The library will highlight books that have been the targets of censorship. These books include *Huckleberry Finn* and *The Catcher in the Rye.*

Activity 2

Sample answer: The feature lists and pictures several local authors and their works.

Lesson 2 Your Turn (p. 17)

For instructor evaluation, use the rubric on p. vi. For student evaluation, use the Peer Review Checklist on p. 111.

Model Level 5 Response:

I understand that some people in this office would like to ask for a raise as a group. Although in some circumstances there is strength in numbers, this is not one of them. If someone feels he or she is worthy of more money, it would be best for this person to address the issue individually with our manager. When it comes to specific issues like hours, pay, and job descriptions, each of us is different and should be treated as such.

Although some might like to believe that we are all the same in this office, this is not really true. Some people have been working here for more than two years, while one person started just three months ago. When it comes to salary, experience counts. Someone who has been here longer should be eligible for a raise before a newer employee.

In addition, our tasks are not exactly the same either. Although we all make sales calls, I also research new leads, which not everyone does. Some others help train new employees, which I do not do. If people's job descriptions are different, it makes sense that their pay might differ as well.

Perhaps most important, I believe that some people in our group are deserving of a raise while others are not, simply based on job performance. Why should we all get the same raise when some of us work harder, get better results, and produce more profits for the company?

For these three reasons, asking for a group raise is not a good idea. Each of us has different experience, different job descriptions, and different levels of performance. We therefore should get paid differently as well.

Lesson 3 Try It (p. 20)

Activity 1

You may classify details differently. The important thing is to be able to identify details that support the main idea.

1. Sample answers— Example: "I am willing to do it every other Monday." Fact: "dirty dishes left on the table every day." Reason: "it is not the job of maintenance to clean up after us."

2. Sample answers—Example: "recently we had to fire a representative who spoke rudely." Fact: "his tone cost the company business, as the customer canceled an order." Reason: "if he or she treats the customer with disrespect or negativity, the customer is not being served well."

Activity 2

Sample detail: In her previous job, she proved herself to be highly organized and attentive to details—two qualities necessary for this position.

Lesson 3 Your Turn (p. 21)

For instructor evaluation, use the rubric on p. vi. For student evaluation, use the Peer Review Checklist on p. 111.

Model Level 5 Response:

It is clear to all of us in the department that there is more work than can be accomplished in an 8-hour day. One solution is to hire another worker; the other solution is to work a longer day to get the job done. I'd like to state my preference for allowing me to work a nine-hour day. I am able and willing to do so, and I believe that an additional worker would not be as productive.

Because I live close to the office and have few commitments outside of work, I am ideally suited to take on this extra work. In fact, my evening management class will be ending at the end of this week, so I could almost immediately take on additional responsibility. As my last review stated, my work has consistently been excellent, and there is no reason that it would not continue to be excellent in a longer day.

Hiring an additional employee to get the work done may at first seem like a good idea; however, consider the training that would need to take place in order to get that person up to speed. It would make sense that I would be the worker to do this training as I am the person who knows the system best. Therefore, it is likely that the company would end up paying <u>both</u> me <u>and</u> the new worker for the same amount of work for at least a while, which is not exactly cutting costs.

It is clear that this additional work should be done by the person who is most familiar with it and who has already demonstrated the ability to do it. Rather than training a whole new employee, it would be wise to simply give me a longer day in which to get the job done.

Lesson 4 Try It (p. 24)

Activity 1

1. Main idea: The new work schedule has had a beneficial effect on employee performance. Extraneous detail: Most employees would like to have the option of working through lunch.

2. Main idea: Customer complaints have increased over the past quarter ending in August. Extraneous detail: Many employees were on vacation during this past quarter.

3. Main idea: Our investigation determined that the five-car accident on Highway 30 had several causes. Extraneous detail: This time of year can be very treacherous on the highways.

Activity 2

The home at 312 Front Street has several areas of damage caused by the recent hurricane. The roof of this building was completely torn off by the high winds. A tree in the front yard was uprooted, striking the front bay window. Siding on the east side of the building was partially ripped off, and flying debris also damaged the garage door.

Lesson 4 Your Turn (p. 25)

For instructor evaluation, use the rubric on p. vi. For student evaluation, use the Peer Review Checklist on p. 111.

Model Level 5 Response:

Beginning our workday at 8:00 instead of 9:00 in the morning is an excellent idea. The earlier start fits into most of our schedules better, people are indeed more productive earlier in the day, and getting out of work at 4:00 instead of 5:00 benefits family life.

Over the past year, I have noticed that most people in the office arrive earlier than 9:00. In my own case, I arrive early because I take my son to school at 7:30 and then come directly to work. I am usually at my counter by 8:00 at the latest. I believe an 8:00 start time would work similarly well with almost all working parents.

In addition, as you point out, people do seem to be more productive earlier in the day. I find it easier to be pleasant to customers and to accomplish more when I have the extra energy of the morning. I have noticed that many of us get worn down and in need of a longer coffee break by late afternoon. The company and our customers would benefit from more energetic workers.

Finally, getting out of work at 4:00 instead of 5:00 would enable me to see some of my son's sporting events and to meet with his teachers after school if need be. I believe that all parents would appreciate this extra time with their children. For those employees without children, they could use this additional hour for exercise, errands, or hobbies.

Thank you for considering this change in our workday hours. The benefits to both our work and our personal lives would far exceed any drawbacks.

Lesson 5 Try It (p. 30)

Activity 1

1. Supporting sentence. Sample revision: Many of our employees are new and are still struggling with current technology.

2. Topic sentence. Sample revision: We are happy to announce a change in the paid holiday schedule.

3. Concluding sentence. Sample revision: I hope these dates are satisfactory and will be approved.

Activity 2

The following start-up procedure must be followed to avoid any loss of data or damage to the system. First, make sure that the light on the surge protector line is on. You'll see the power switch on the computer tower is located on the front panel. Press it firmly.

It will turn red when pressed, indicating it is on. The machine will then boot up after a few seconds. Be sure you press the power light located on the monitor to turn it on. When the machine boots, you will see a prompt to enter your password. Enter it. Your screen will then appear. Start up is complete.

Lesson 5 Your Turn (p. 31)

For instructor evaluation, use the rubric on p. vi. For student evaluation, use the Peer Review Checklist on p. 111.

Model Level 5 Response:

While I agree that people are not paying attention to many important memos, the solution to require printing them out is not a good one. Printed memos often go unread as well, and this overuse of paper is not in keeping with our organization's goal to be as eco-friendly as possible. We need to find a better solution to the problem of unread memos.

There is a consensus in the office that we all receive too many e-mails that do not apply to us. For example, we do not need to receive e-mails regarding shipping and receiving because we do not deal with that department. Also, we are copied on e-mails from the childcare site even though many of us don't have a child in the program. If we were able to reduce the number of e-mails coming to us, we could do a better job of paying attention to the important ones that apply to us.

In terms of paper usage, last year our department made a commitment to reducing paper waste and increasing recycling efforts. By all measures, we have done a great job of this. In fact, the e-mail system we have in place has helped us reach our goals in this area. If we return to printing out e-mails, we will be going back to the waste we have worked so hard to reduce.

I am hopeful that we can find a different solution to the e-mail problem. Perhaps by reducing the number of e-mails we receive and paying better attention to the ones we get, we can continue to be the eco-friendly department we are committed to being.

Lesson 6 Try It (p. 34)

Activity 1

Whenever sales drop dramatically, a company must take drastic steps. Unfortunately, our company experienced a steep drop in sales (20%) of school products during the previous quarter. Several factors are the cause.

Activity 2

Productivity is a concern and a goal. Our team recently conducted a study to identify the key factor or factors that contribute to employee productivity. The results were quite interesting.

Lesson 6 Your Turn (p. 35)

For instructor evaluation, use the rubric on p. vi. For student evaluation, use the Peer Review Checklist on p. 111.

Model Level 5 Response:

What organizational style—team or individual—would work best for our company and its employees? That question can be answered by experience, which has shown that even though each of us might be doing a satisfactory job, if we do not work together, we will fall short of our goals. Teamwork is the answer, not individual action.

Last month, a good example of how lack of teamwork affected productivity occurred. Each worker was busy and focused on fulfilling his or her own customer orders. In fact, each worker was so focused on individual orders that none of us paid attention to the dwindling supply of forms. As a result, we were out of order forms by Wednesday and had to use much less efficient ways to write up orders for the rest of the week, until a new supply was delivered on Monday. In addition, some employees blamed others for using "their" forms or for not noticing the dwindling supply and taking action to order more.

If we had considered ourselves a team rather than individual employees, we would have been paying more attention to the stockpile, knowing that the more each used, the fewer there would be for others. We would invent a better system for taking stock of the inventory and for ordering more forms. Had we worked together as a team, we could have solved the problem before it became a problem.

This incident is just one of many examples of how individualism can hurt the company and how teamwork will net greater profitability. Let's start working as a team to avoid the problems of the past.

Lesson 7 Try It (p. 38)

Activity 1

Allowing telecommuting, then, would result in increased productivity due to saved time and less stress. Telecommuting is a policy that benefits employees and management.

Activity 2

Because of their income, credit rating, and absence of debt, therefore, Mr. and Mrs. Rogers present a good risk for our company. I hereby recommend them for a mortgage loan, with the terms as listed above.

Lesson 7 Your Turn (p. 39)

For instructor evaluation, use the rubric on p. vi. For student evaluation, use the Peer Review Checklist on p. 111.

Model Level 5 Response:

Today it is virtually impossible to identify and legislate every type of human relationship there is. For example, can two people be friends without being a couple? What about two people who used to be a couple—can they now be friends? Because of the complexities of human relationships, and because it is a question of individual freedom as well, it is pointless for this company to try to tell employees with whom they can and cannot socialize or be in a relationship.

Long ago, it was perhaps easier to determine the status of the relationship between two people. It was therefore much easier for a company to establish a "no dating" policy. Although people could be friendly within the office walls, it was understood that "dating"—an exclusive, romantic relationship between a man and a woman—was not allowed. In the 21st century, however, there is no such easy delineation of relationships. Research tells us that formal dating is more rare, and casual yet intimate relationships are on the rise. Which kind do you forbid?

Just as important is the issue of personal freedom. As long as employees perform their jobs satisfactorily, what they do outside the workplace is no one's business but their own. Company policy should reflect employees' ability to separate work and personal life. In fact, there is no need to assume that any personal relationship is necessarily a threat to the workplace. Over time, people have grown more skilled at understanding and managing the nuances of workplace relationships. People know the pitfalls of dating the boss; they recognize the rewards of keeping their private lives private when it comes to office politics.

The bottom line is that employees are either good performers on the job or they are not. Some people who keep their personal lives completely separate from the job still lack integrity, dedication, and intelligence when it comes to the workplace. Other people who maintain personal and intimate relationships with coworkers turn out to be the best employees in the company. Setting policy around this complex issue is neither wise nor beneficial to our business.

Lesson 8 Try It (p. 42)

Activity 1

Sample transitions: staffing plan. <u>At that time,</u> current employees. . . . if possible. <u>However,</u> some complaints. . . . and resolution.

<u>Initially,</u> I anticipate. . . . <u>In addition,</u> older employees. . . . <u>Similarly,</u> long-term. . . .

<u>Nevertheless,</u> the two. . . .procedures. <u>With their ability and experience,</u> regular training seminars and weekly staff meetings should alleviate most of these problems.

Activity 2

The first paragraph opens with the main idea and uses the word *first,* which tells the reader a sequence of events will follow. The second sentence begins with the transition word *Then* that signals this sentence will contain the next step in the process. The following sentence tells the reader where to locate the information on "long side and short side" mentioned in the previous sentences. The second paragraph uses the transition word *now* that connects ideas between the two paragraphs. The last sentence begins with the word *Therefore,* signaling the relation to the previous sentence.

Lesson 8 Your Turn (p. 43)

For instructor evaluation, use the rubric on p. vi. For student evaluation, use the Peer Review Checklist on p. 111.

Model Level 5 Response:

A new position offers the chance to develop varied experience and new skills. While I usually welcome such opportunity, my preference at this time is to stay in my current position. I have thought long and hard about the pros and cons of each option and have decided that it would be best both for me and for the company if I continue to do the work I have started.

From a personal perspective, keeping my current job has several advantages. First of all, it would allow me to avoid the stress that comes with a new position. I have small children, and it is important that I arrive home at the end of the day with some energy and a positive outlook. In addition, if I stay in my current job, I will be eligible for a raise sooner than if I take the new position. Finally, from a career standpoint, there are several aspects of my current job that I have yet to explore. I feel that I can gain valuable new experience and grow as an employee in my current job.

From the perspective of what is best for the company, I also believe the status quo is the best option. As I stated above, I am able to do my job efficiently and productively. Contributing to the company's success means staying where I am, I believe. The time, money, and effort it would take to find and train a new employee would be wasted.

I hope you agree with this analysis and allow me to stay in my current position—confident, productive, and stress-free—both for my good and the good of the company.

Lesson 9 Try It (p. 48)

Activity 1

1. Prices for new uniforms will increase next month.

2. Employees who wear blue jeans to work violate the dress code.

3. OK

4. Your claim that your training service creates positive learning experiences for new employees has not proved true in our case.

5. Because of the tight schedule and rigid deadlines, employees must work at the office every day instead of telecommuting one day each week.

Activity 2

(1) "It has some strong features that will <u>bowl over</u> our client" uses informal language. *It has some strong features that will excite our client.* (2) "I also like the <u>cool</u> pictures" has slang. *I also like the inventive visuals.* (3) "The image of the laughing clown holding his sides is <u>as old as the hills</u> and <u>makes me cringe</u>" uses a cliche and informal, rude language. *The image of the laughing clown holding his sides is stale and should be replaced.*

Lesson 9 Your Turn (p. 49)

For instructor evaluation, use the rubric on p. vi. For student evaluation, use the Peer Review Checklist on p. 111.

Model Lesson 5 Response:

Should we hire an administrative assistant to take notes at our meetings? The answer is yes, and for three good reasons: low cost, preemptive action to avoid problems, and greater productivity as a group.

Regarding cost, our group meets once a week for two hours; therefore, we would need to pay a note-taker for approximately 10 hours per month, including two hours per month for copying and circulating the notes after each meeting. At the going rate of $10 per hour, note-taker fees would not exceed $100 per month. Divided among ten of us, that comes to only $10 per month—a very small price to pay for greater convenience and productivity.

If we were to decide to rotate the note-taking task among the group, consider some of the problems that might arise. For example, what happens if the designated note-taker is late or absent? How would we handle a situation where the quality of the notes varied widely? These are just two issues that might cause problems that hinder our work.

Most importantly, our discussions are valuable and complex enough that we want and need each and every member's undivided attention at every meeting. An important thought might be missed if the note-taker is focused on writing down the previous person's comment. My experience with note-taking is that the task, though not particularly difficult, prevents one from being free to jump in with ideas and questions.

We must seriously consider hiring an administrative assistant to help us with our important task. We can do so at little expense, we will avoid unexpected headaches, and we will get the full benefit of all our voices at every meeting.

Lesson 10 Try It (p. 52)

Activity 1

1. The paintings and sculptures in the museum are priceless.

2. Most employees believe that parties after work improve morale.

3. New employees need to understand the benefits our company offers.

4. All managers must analyze our competitors' new products.

5. It was grossly unfair for her to be passed over for promotion.

Activity 2

Our new exhibit, *The Age of Elizabeth*, will open in January of next year. It will <u>display</u> many of the <u>antique</u> printed books and rare artifacts in our collection. The exhibit will especially be <u>appreciated</u> by teachers and students of British history and literature. It will allow them to <u>study</u> letters in Queen Elizabeth's own handwriting and to <u>view</u> first editions of several of Shakespeare's plays as well as those of his contemporaries. To <u>launch</u> the exhibit, I would like you to <u>present</u> an overview for our first-night audience.

Lesson 10 Your Turn (p. 53)

For instructor evaluation, use the rubric on p. vi. For student evaluation, use the Peer Review Checklist on p. 111.

Model Level 5 Response:

I commend our company for encouraging employees to improve their English language and business writing skills. Such a policy can only give our company a competitive edge and so benefit us all. However, effective business writing is a skill, like any other, that requires training. Because our company provides training for every other skill it expects employees to acquire, it needs to provide business writing classes in the workplace.

Workers who have been hired by this company were offered employment based on their existing talents, skills, experience, and work ethic. Clearly, management believed that they could do their jobs with the skills they had, and they were right. Our company has been quite productive using the labor of its employees.

When a task arose for which a worker was not qualified or proficient in, management always gave the worker a choice—get trained, move to another department, or leave the company. If a worker chose to be trained, classes and on-the-job coaching were provided on-site. In no case was a worker expected to find training elsewhere. Through this process, employees continually improved their skills, and the company benefited.

Business writing proficiency should be attained with exactly this model. Everyone agrees that this skill will improve the productivity and efficiency of the workers. Ultimately, the company benefits enormously. Yet if workers have to expend time, energy, and money finding high quality classes that are convenient and accessible, no one will benefit.

The company does not make its assembly workers find quality control training outside the workplace. Why should business writing training be any different?

Lesson 11 Try It (p. 58)

Activity 1

1. Option B is correct. The sentence is complete and flows smoothly. Option A includes a sentence fragment. Option C has an awkward opening phrase.

2. *First, the main problem* is the sentence fragment. Option A is the correct revision.

Activity 2

The study on growing *E.coli* in three different media has been jeopardized by an incident that occurred on March 19. The incident began when a flaw was discovered in the glove worn by a lab technician. When the flaw, a small hole previously unnoticed, was discovered, the technician immediately changed gloves. However, he had previously handled sample 3, and it may have been contaminated. Because of this possible contamination, the experiment will need to be repeated.

Lesson 11 Your Turn (p. 59)

For instructor evaluation, use the rubric on p. vi. For student evaluation, use the Peer Review Checklist on p. 111.

Model Level 5 Response:

Health insurance and sick pay are essential for workers' well-being, both physical and financial. Even so, I agree with the company's policy to hire as many part-time workers as possible without these benefits. There are two good reasons for keeping this policy, even though it might be unpopular with some workers.

The first reason to hold onto our current employees at 30-hours per week can best be understood by looking at what would happen if we did not do so. For example, suppose we laid off half of our part-time employees so that the other half could receive health benefits. The company's productivity would go down due to a smaller workforce. Stress levels would rise, people would need to work longer hours, and the company would suffer. In addition, the half of the workforce that was let go would still not have health insurance, nor would they have an income to feed, clothe, and house their families. The net impact on the lives of both the employed and the no-longer-employed would be negative.

The second reason to keep the current policy is that doing so will help the business grow so that eventually all workers will be employed with health benefits. Company management has determined that having a greater number of part-time employees is more efficient and productive than having a smaller number of full-time employees. However, management has not said that this model is a permanent one; instead, it is doing what it needs to do in order to keep the business viable now. The more profitable the company becomes, the more full-time workers it can afford to hire.

I realize that this position is not a popular one, especially for those part-time employees who are struggling to pay medical bills. However, I ask them to persevere and accept part-time work in the short term. In the long term, both they and the company as a whole will benefit.

Lesson 12 Try It (p. 62)

Activity 1

1. This year's annual sales meeting will be held at Royal Hotel in New Orleans. As the meeting's social coordinator, I have planned a series of activities that should please all tastes. Details will be announced as soon as we finalize them. Anyone who has suggestions may call or e-mail me.

2. Our company is considering changing insurance providers. We would like you to submit a bid. We have 35 employees, but only one has a family. He has three young children. We want medical coverage for employees and owners, and we also want to include dental insurance. Please send your bid before October 1. Call me if you have questions.

3. As many of you know, we will be installing a new computer system on November 1. Training will begin as soon as installation is complete. The new system will make communications within the company easier and faster. There will be less down time. We think you will be pleased with the change.

Activity 2

The conditions at Plant 31 are generally up to code. I did observe minor problems, but there was only one important one. In building 5, area 12, pump valve handles appear to be wearing and should be replaced. Repeat inspection will be necessary. This is a minor problem, but it could develop into a serious hazard. We should schedule another inspection within three months.

Lesson 12 Your Turn (p. 63)

For instructor evaluation, use the rubric on p. vi. For student evaluation, use the Peer Review Checklist on p. 111.

Model Level 5 Response:

It is not fair to compensate employees for an activity outside of work, especially when that activity requires special skill. Although it can be argued that a day off is not compensation and that no skill is needed to play softball, I respectfully disagree on both counts.

In the business world, we receive wages for the hours we work. The company is now proposing to give team members additional time off. Who will be doing the work of these employees on that day? And won't the dollars wasted in this loss of productivity need to be made up somehow? Our company is based on the premise that it pays for work—work that will end up earning the company a profit. Yet playing softball does not result in profit; in fact, it actually lowers profits because it is unproductive "work."

In addition, not everyone can participate in an after-hours softball league. Has management considered the seven physically disabled employees? Furthermore, what considerations are being made for the employees who have second jobs to get to or who have serious family commitments at the end of a workday?

The fact of the matter is that the people who will benefit from this league are young, able-bodied people without families—a small fraction of the company workforce. Many older, less-able-bodied workers would love an opportunity to "earn" an extra day off. Until you come up with a plan to accommodate these workers as well, I encourage you to abandon the softball team idea.

Lesson 13 Try It (p. 66)

Activity 1

1. Although it is true that we have planned reorganization, rumors about job loss are unfounded. . . . Those with a technical background are most likely to be moved to a new team that deals only with technical issues.

2. When the organization plan is finally in place.

3. When the organization plan is finally in place, most employees will remain in their current positions.

Activity 2

<u>Because</u> corn has been highly bred over the centuries, it currently has a small base of genes.

Because the world climate is changing, a new breed of corn that can adapt to a changing world is important.

Lesson 13 Your Turn (p. 67)

For instructor evaluation, use the rubric on p. vi. For student evaluation, use the Peer Review Checklist on p. 111.

Model Level 5 Response:

We as a work team need to make some decisions about the use of the refrigerator and stick to them. Maintenance does not need this additional headache, nor do we. We are all too busy to worry about whether our lunches will be there when we want them or whether the refrigerator will be a disgusting mess on a Monday morning. I propose three simple rules to solve this problem.

First, let's set a cleaning schedule and task list for each week of the month. Eight of us use the refrigerator, so each of us will be responsible for cleaning only one week out of every two months. We can post the schedule in the break room. Weekly tasks should include throwing out leftovers every Friday and wiping down shelves as needed.

Second, I recommend that the bottom shelf be designated as "shared." If you bring a bottle of salad dressing and you don't mind if someone else uses it, put it on the bottom shelf. If your department has leftover birthday cake to share, put it on the bottom shelf. Of course, this implies that anything on the other four shelves is meant only for personal use. Salad dressing on the second shelf means "Do Not Touch" unless you are the owner. Leftover birthday cake on the top shelf means that you plan to finish it later or that you are saving it to take home.

Finally, we should all show respect for our hardworking colleagues. It's easy, of course, to "borrow" some ketchup even if it is on the second shelf. And if you see your favorite cookies on the top shelf, you may think it "won't matter" if you have "just one." However, if we all keep in mind how it feels to have someone disrespect <u>our</u> property, we will likely think twice before we do the same to someone else.

Lesson 14 Try It (p. 70)

Activity 1

1. We also have specials on this year's popular toys, as well as holiday items and clothing.

2. We will open our doors at 4:00 A.M. and expect all employees to report by 3:30 A.M.

3. Frustrated by the crowd, customers will have short tempers.

4. Even so, we will not tolerate any rudeness to our customers. Extra security guards will be on duty, so report any problems to them immediately.

Activity 2

The center of the wolf's life is the pack. The "lone wolf" is not a happy wolf. The pack is its family and its society. The pack has a leader and followers, and each wolf knows its place in the pack.

Because wolves range across a wide area while hunting, they often get separated. While humans keep in touch across miles by phone, letters, and Internet, wolves have a unique way of communicating with the family. They howl. Just as every human has a unique voice, every wolf has a unique howl that is recognized by pack members. The wolf howl carries over great distances. The sound can travel across a tundra and through a forest. The howl calls the pack together.

Lesson 14 Your Turn (p. 71)

For instructor evaluation, use the rubric on p. vi. For student evaluation, use the Peer Review Checklist on p. 111.

Model Level 5 Response:

We all want a safe and healthy workplace, but mandating personal health care decisions is not the best way to achieve this goal. Requiring flu vaccines is actually just a shortcut to creating a healthy work environment, and ultimately it will prove to be an ineffective one. The best way to ensure healthy workers is to educate them and support them in their decisions.

Research has shown that when people are in charge of their own health care decisions, they tend to take better care of themselves. Suppose you force a worker to get the flu vaccine, and he does so against his will just so that he can keep his job. Now think about all the other decisions this worker has to make to keep himself healthy. Will he stop smoking? Will he see a physician regularly? Will he cut down on sugars and fats? Will he exercise more? The answers to all of these questions is "maybe" at best. It is possible, actually, that the worker will be so angry about the mandated flu vaccine that he in essence "sabotages" his health just to prove a point.

Now consider the alternative. Instead of mandating the flu vaccine, you educate the employee about how to maintain a healthy lifestyle. One way is to get a flu shot, a proven-effective strategy to avoid a very uncomfortable and often dangerous illness. In addition, you mention other ways to become and stay healthy—all of those mentioned above. You tell this employee that you respect his decision-making skills and that you trust he will choose the optimum way to care for his health.

It is my strong belief that the latter strategy will result in more employees getting the vaccine. Even better, it will result in more employees making other healthy changes to their lifestyles.

Lesson 15 Try It (p. 76)

Activity 1

1. OK

2. Mr. Taylor and Mr. Higgins has worked; Mr. Taylor and Mr. Higgins, offensive coach and defensive coach respectively, have worked out a practice schedule.

3. Funds is intended; Funds from this increase are intended for a new roof on the high school and for a program to update some of the classrooms.

A student representative and a school staff representative is; A student representative and a school staff representative are scheduled to be at each voting site to hand out flyers supporting this initiative.

Activity 2

biomaterials and nanotechnology are . . . .These materials have. . . . Materials technology currently in use does not promote. . . .An increase in R&D funds is. . . .

Lesson 15 Your Turn (p. 77)

For instructor evaluation, use the rubric on p. vi. For student evaluation, use the Peer Review Checklist on p. 111.

Model Level 5 Response:

Vacation time is not a gift or a reward from a company to its employees; rather, it is earned time that is owed to the employee. The current "no-rollover" policy disrespects the work employees perform and therefore jeopardizes their productivity. It should be changed to allow workers to bank their vacation time.

While accumulated vacation days might put a strain on planning for some departments, this is not reason enough to take away a basic employee right. It is true that if Joe Jones does not take a vacation for two years and then decides to take four weeks off in the middle of budget season, there will be stress on the accounting department. However, those two weeks belong to Joe Jones, not to the company. The company benefited from the 340 days per year that Joe worked for two years straight; it benefited from his not taking any days off. Now the company will need to figure out a way to give Joe what he is owed—without penalty.

Another major reason to change this company's vacation policy is that sooner or later it will begin to affect worker morale and productivity. For example, one warehouse worker has not taken any vacation time because his family lives in the Dominican Republic, and it is too far to go for just ten days. Rather than take time off to just stay at home, he keeps hoping that company policy will change so that he can take a vacation with real value to him. He would like to see his family for a month in the Dominican Republic. If we keep denying him this right to use the time he has earned, he may become bitter and unproductive. Or worse, he could quit, and the company would lose one of its most dedicated and trusted workers.

It is gratifying that the company is considering changing this unfair vacation policy and allowing employees to use their earned time as they see fit. If you do change, you will be respecting the rights of your workers and will be more likely to keep excellent workers happy and productive.

Lesson 16 Try It (p. 80)

Activity 1

1. OK

2. I had hoped we could use the current training materials, but since we now have a new department, we have done some extensive revision on the program.

3. The Newton Institute has been training people for careers in the trades and technology since 1987. Although our name has changed, our mission remains the same today as always.

Activity 2

Dear Mr. Huffstedt:

Our team recently <u>visited</u> your plant.... which <u>could reduce</u> the environmental impact of your manufacturing process as well.

... we <u>will systematically eliminate</u> waste in eight areas....

...After we <u>have</u> an initial chat....

Lesson 16 Your Turn (p. 81)

For instructor evaluation, use the rubric on p. vi. For student evaluation, use the Peer Review Checklist on p. 111.

Model Level 5 Response:

Every working shift has its pluses and minuses. Ask a 9–5 employee what he or she thinks of these work hours, and you will hear both good and bad. Similarly, evening shift workers might like some aspects of their hours and dislike others. For this reason, it is unfair to treat "graveyard shift" workers any differently or to award them any special privileges.

The 9–5 shift is desirable because you work the hours that most employees in the country work. These workers "fit in" with the majority. However, these same workers might find it difficult to do business with organizations that have the same hours. For example, how does a 9–5 employee visit the dentist or see her child's teacher? The answer is—with difficulty. Because our professionals, government offices, and schools run on this same schedule, it can be a challenge to coordinate activities between them. Lunch hours turn into "errand hours," during which 9–5 employees rush around taking care of personal business.

The downside of the 5–1 shift is probably obvious. If you have a family, you have no evening time with them, and they are asleep when you return home. There is no such thing as a family dinner. On the plus side, you have plenty of time during day hours to get errands done, pick children up from school, and enjoy the daylight.

The late-shift employees have stated their objections to their hours. Because public transportation is not available, they need to find other ways to get to work. While this is indeed an inconvenience, consider the upside of this shift as well. First of all, there is no traffic, something that the other two shifts struggle with every day. Second, people who work this shift can sleep in the morning and still enjoy a full day of activity. They can drive their kids to school <u>and</u> pick them up. They can have dinner with their families as well.

No public transportation is indeed a negative aspect of the late shift, but that disadvantage is no more compelling than the downsides of any other shift. Every employee has to choose a shift and accept its drawbacks without expecting special compensation.

Lesson 17 Try It (p. 84)

Activity 1

1. However, we were surprised to get a phone call yesterday complaining that one of our representatives was rude to the caller in a recent conversation.

2. OK

3. OK

4. Traffic will be diverted to Hanley Avenue.

Activity 2

However, my tests show that a new design in the electrodes <u>is</u> needed as soon as possible to handle this additional electrical charge. In addition, field tests will be needed at some point to ensure that patients <u>are</u> able to tolerate the higher levels.

Lesson 17 Your Turn (p. 85)

For instructor evaluation, use the rubric on p. vi. For student evaluation, use the Peer Review Checklist on p. 111.

Model Level 5 Response:

Forcing people to retire at age 60 is not only an insult to the employees you have relied on for years, but it also is a flawed strategy that will result in both short- and long-term harm to this company. Rather than lowering the average age of your employees, I recommend finding new ways to make <u>all</u> workers more productive.

Both men and women in their sixties, and even seventies, have been working hard in this company for many years. They have contributed enormously to growing this business from a small one-office operation to a large, multi-city enterprise. I can't imagine this company being what it is today without the work of Pete Johnson, Manuel Tabares, or Nancy Duffy. While some people lose their productivity as they age, surely this cannot be said of these three individuals. We would be a greatly diminished organization without their expertise and efforts.

By lowering the retirement age, the company would be ignoring what research has been telling us for years: The wisdom and experience that come with age are irreplaceable. Although younger people do indeed bring energy, new ideas, and fresh perspectives to the workplace, there is much they cannot provide. For example, at our last department meeting, a 26-year-old recent hire shared an idea for a new product. While his idea seemed promising, it was helpful to hear from Manuel (age 63) that a similar product failed 15 years ago. Had we not had Manuel's perspective, we might have made the same mistake again.

Rather than mandating early retirement, the company could partner younger workers with older workers to take advantage of the usefulness of different ages. If we make sure that every work team and every committee has employees of mixed ages, we enhance their assets and minimize their drawbacks. By valuing both experience and youth, we will be a stronger company overall.

Lesson 18 Try It (p. 88)

Activity 1

1. Me and Mike are going to drive down there to investigate it. *Me is an object pronoun; the antecedent to it is unclear. Mike and I are going to drive down there to investigate the violations.*

2. A child living in an older building often ingests it, causing serious developmental damage to them. *Them is the wrong number. A child living in an older building often ingests it, causing serious developmental damage to himself or herself.*

3. We are sending a team of investigators to see if it can be solved, but both the director and me think we will have to issue a citation. *There is no antecedent to it; me is an object pronoun. We are sending a team of investigators to see if the problem can be solved, but both the director and I think we will have to issue a citation.*

4. The primary presenter at the symposium is the assistant director of the EPA, and they will explain the new policy and options for taking advantage of it. *They is the wrong number. The primary presenter at the symposium is the assistant director of the EPA, and he [or she] will explain the new policy and options for taking advantage of it.*

Activity 2

. . . Mr. Grey will need to be prepared with a list of personal items that Mr. and Mrs. Clark contest. . . . as the list of items must be filed with the petition. Please send a copy of the list to Mr. Brown and me. . . .

Lesson 18 Your Turn (p. 89)

For instructor evaluation, use the rubric on p. vi. For student evaluation, use the Peer Review Checklist on p. 111.

Model Level 5 Response:

As anyone who occasionally notices the trash containers in our building knows, we are doing an inadequate job in our reducing, reusing, and recycling efforts. I propose we do three things to keep us on track and be more of a "green" company.

First, to reduce our use of paper, plastic, and aluminum, we could remind employees to bring their lunches in plastic containers instead of plastic or paper bags. All employees could agree to print out fewer e-mails and reports and to rely on electronic versions as much as possible. Finally, let's ask catering to stop ordering from those companies that overpackage our breakfast and lunch orders. Every week, we throw away multiple bags and boxes due to overwrapping.

Second, before employees throw away paper or plastic, office posters can remind them to ask themselves, "How can I reuse this?" One idea is to reverse sides and reuse $8\frac{1}{2}$ by 11 paper in both the printer and the copier. Another way to reuse paper is to shred it and then send it down to the warehouse for packing material. Quite a bit of scrap paper can be reused in this way.

Finally, we can improve our recycling signs and bins. Currently, if employees want to recycle paper, they must walk up a flight of stairs to the bin in the office administrator's office. If we put new, eye-catching recycling bins next to every copy machine and printer, we will increase our recycling amount by 100%.

Reduce, reuse, and recycle. If we make these three efforts as easy as possible, we will let workers know that we are serious about being green.

Lesson 19 Try It (p. 92)

Activity 1

1. *its* zoom; turn off the camera and press; red light was on, I

2. Every floor worker and every supervisor; Wear casual, comfortable, and cool clothes; we will be. . . . I'll be at the front office. . . . together. The more. . . . will get done.

Activity 2

an electrical power summary, a complete computer update assessment, and an emergency response test. . . . 8-hour period, and all. . . .next 8 hours. This check. . . . reliability. We're pleased to report. . . .

Lesson 19 Your Turn (p. 93)

For instructor evaluation, use the rubric on p. vi. For student evaluation, use the Peer Review Checklist on p. 111.

Model Level 5 Response:

The company should continue its current maternity/paternity leave policies. In other words, mothers and fathers should continue to receive six weeks of paid leave, following which they can either come back to work or take more time without pay. Although this might seem harsh, especially when compared with the more generous European plans, this is really the maximum the company can afford without harming itself and the rest of its employees.

Six weeks is enough time for parents to bond with their newborn. Study after study shows that by this age, infants are able to distinguish a parent's voice among other voices in the room. He or she has begun to prefer the parent over other caregivers. And most often, the 6-week-old infant has established a reliable sleep/wake pattern, as well as a regular feeding schedule. Although no one would argue that this is an easy or convenient time for a parent to go back to work, this timing will not affect the baby any more than an 8- or 10- or 12-week departure.

Some might argue a newborn and a parent need more bonding time. If this is the opinion of the new parent, he or she is welcome to take unpaid leave in the form of vacation. This is where the fairness issue arises. While I respect the dedication shown by an increasing number of new parents, we cannot favor this population over any others. What about the other end of the life cycle? What favors does the company grant to employees caring for sick and dying parents? We are all welcome to take vacation time or unpaid leave to do what is necessary to care for our families—whether that be an infant or an elderly person.

If the company were to offer more paid maternity and/or paternity leave, in fairness it would be necessary to offer paid leave for elder care or other family needs. We would all quickly find ourselves out of a job because the company could no longer afford to employ nonworkers and keep up with its other financial obligations. Please keep the standing maternity/paternity policy.

Lesson 20 Try It (p. 96)

Activity 1

1. two; know; coming

2. believe; would; advisable; new; regulations

3. It's; employees; wear; for

4. whether; your; attending

Activity 2

I am **writing** this letter. . . . There are **two** ways. . . .the **outstanding** balance. . . . calling **our** credit department to make **arrangements** for. . . . you have **received** this letter. . . . risk **becoming** a **discredited** customer. If this were **to** happen. . . . place **your** orders. . . .be **paid**. . . .

Lesson 20 Your Turn (p. 97)

For instructor evaluation, use the rubric on p. vi. For student evaluation, use the Peer Review Checklist on p. 111.

Model Level 5 Response:

Like it or not, the Internet has now become our standard form of connecting to the world, and our company needs to keep up with the times and embrace this connection in a realistic and fair manner. Management has trusted employees to make decisions around telephone use, office conversations, coffee breaks, and other "nonproductive" use of time. Management should now trust us with balanced Internet usage. If it does not, I predict that efficiency and productivity will in fact go down.

We are all trusted to keep our break room chit-chat to a minimum. We know that hanging out by the vending machines is not only a waste of our own time, but also a waste of company resources. This is why you do not see people in the break room for hours on end—they're too busy getting their work done. Similarly, we use the telephone for personal calls that help us stay productive on the job. We call a son's daycare center to say we're running late. We call a spouse or friend to ask for a favor. We phone ahead to make sure a car repair place is open before we take the time to drive over there. Without wise and fair use of the telephone, our efficiency and productivity would decrease due to worry, stress, and poor planning.

The company would be wise to view Internet usage as a simple extension of the employee's ability to manage personal tasks without taking unfair advantage of the situation. Of course, there will always be a handful of workers who abuse the privilege of Internet access, just as they do with break time and personal telephone calls. But we cannot make policies based on the unscrupulous actions of these few. As a whole, this company's employees have acted with integrity, and our profits have reflected this.

Without Internet access, employees will not be able to quickly send an e-mail to a spouse, asking him/her to check in on a sick child or parent. We would also not be able to do a search for a competent plumber to fix an overflowing sink—and therefore might have to take time off for the task. A simple reminder to workers that idly surfing the Web is the equivalent of hanging out by the vending machines will be enough to keep up the productivity and efficiency of the company.

Lesson 21 Try It (p. 100)

Activity 1

1. OK

2. Professor

3. OK

Activity 2

Monday; Dr. Mendoza; north section of the city; medical building; Street; Drive; Web

Lesson 21 Your Turn (p. 101)

For instructor evaluation, use the rubric on p. vi. For student evaluation, use the Peer Review Checklist on p. 111.

Model Level 5 Response:

Smokers have been complaining about the distance they now need to walk in order to have a cigarette during their workday. Nonsmokers are now complaining that they spend more time on the job than smokers. The best way to solve this dilemma is to give all workers a specified amount of time for their breaks and allow them to use the time however they wish.

Although some people have a real distaste for the cigarette habit, they cannot take away fellow employees' rights to smoke, as long as it is done off workplace grounds. New regulations require that smokers walk over three hundred yards away from the building to have a cigarette, and the company needs to make accommodations so that smokers can satisfy their personal needs. People who oppose such accommodations should consider the issue of bathroom usage. Employees who need to use the facilities more often than others are not penalized for the extra time they take away from their jobs. Smokers should not be penalized either.

However, allowing this extra time to smokers will create unnecessary inequities in the workplace unless nonsmokers are allowed the same amount of break time. It stands to reason that employees should not receive less break time just because they do not smoke.

The most equitable solution is to give <u>all</u> employees thirty minutes of break time each day. Smokers can easily take a walk and smoke a cigarette twice during this allotted time. Nonsmokers can take two 15-minute breaks or one 30-minute break, depending on their own preferences. This policy is simple and easy to implement immediately, and it works for smokers and nonsmokers alike.